In memory of Prince Rogers Nelson, 1958–2016

Wax Poetics
Issue 50
Special Edition Reprint
Originally published January 2012

© 2016 Wax Poetics
ISBN 978-0-9798110-6-7

Front cover and opposite photo by Allen Beaulieu.
Back cover photo by Julian Berman.

Wax Poetics Books | www.waxpoeticsbooks.com
Printed in the USA by Lightning Source | www.lightningsource.com

Editor-in-Chief
Andre Torres

Editor
Brian DiGenti

Marketing Director
Dennis Coxen

Art Directors
Joshua Dunn
Freddy Anzures

Associate Editor
Tom McClure

Contributing Editor
Andrew Mason

Contributing Writers
Tony Best
Ericka Blount Danois
Michael A. Gonzales
Alan Leeds
Gwen Leeds
Miles Marshall Lewis
David Ma
Andrew Mason
Allen Thayer
Ahmir "Questlove" Thompson
Matthew Trammell
Dean Van Nguyen

Contributing Photographers
Allen Beaulieu
Julian Berman
Shawn Brackbill
Robert Adam Mayer
Jorge Peniche
Michael Putland
Brick Stowell

What you're holding in your hands is pure grind. Blood, sweat, and tears in print. I'm not even going to front, in ten years and fifty issues, it never got so sincerious. This was without a doubt the hardest issue we've ever done. We decided to flip the script, went back to the lab and came up with a new formula—Wax Poetics 2.0, if you will. So we're looking kinda brand new right now, but it feels real good. We took a cue from the man who changed his name to a symbol and did the same. The fresh new logo, size, paper, and redesign were a long time coming; so to celebrate this double milestone, we decided to jump it off. And who better to get on some next shit with than Prince?

It's almost impossible to tell the entire Prince story, but we've wanted to do something for a minute, especially after hearing so many nuggets from his former on-tour/off-tour manager, Alan Leeds. Alan's firsthand account of those pivotal years coming off the *1999* tour through the making of both the *Purple Rain* album and film, and subsequent tour, takes center stage as he recalls intimate moments with help from his then girlfriend and now wife, Gwen. From there, we built it brick by brick—Morris Day, Jesse Johnson, Madhouse, the Family, even Questo wanted to get down. Like the Godfather and the Atomic Dog, Prince is one of those larger-than-life personalities whose story is even better illustrated with the help of those who worked closely with him over the years. This is, by far, not the definitive Prince joint, but we're one step closer to telling the whole story.

Prince could very well be the last great genius of Black music in a tradition that goes back past even Ellington and Armstrong. Whether it was his solo work, or one of his many side hustles like the Time, the Family, Madhouse, Vanity 6, or Sheila E., the Purple One had the game on lock. The perfect synthesis of R&B, funk, rock, pop, jazz, and new wave, Prince carved out the kind of creative space for himself that few others have. Beginning a career fully Afroed at the end of the '70s, Prince was already on his own thang by the '80s and hasn't looked back since. Bringing funk and soul into the next decade and beyond, Prince continues to redefine what it means to be a Black musician, with a swagger often imitated, but never duplicated.

Most still hold Prince's earlier work as the gold standard, and there are a few kids out there channeling that period in their music on some level or another. A handful of young brothas are pushing boundaries and developing their own unique sound. So to mix it up, we gathered a trifecta of cats who are trying to take it somewhere else.

Frank Ocean, Blood Orange, and Toro y Moi represent a new wave of R&B artists that chooses to operate outside the formulaic approach of modern radio. This is R&B for a post-hip-hop generation. A generation who doesn't so neatly categorize music as record labels hope, or even feel the need to own the music they love.

Like Prince before him, Frank Ocean has people wondering. It's fitting that they're both part of paradigm shifts in the industry. Prince was the beginning of the end for major labels back in the mid-'90s, awaking artists to the realization that they don't need majors to connect their music with the people. Not quite two decades later, enter Frank Ocean. His career stifled by major label malaise, he throws an album on Tumblr and within a year is working with Jay and Kanye. Major moves for a kid Def Jam had on the pay-no-mind list. Now they're paying attention, and so is everyone else. Frank's not an easy dude to pin down, but he took the time to sit with us out of respect. So we deliver the finest interview to date on an artist that didn't come to the game, but made the game come to him. And for us, that's what this new musical and cultural landscape is all about.

With this issue, we turn the page on a decade at Wax Poetics and look forward to the next one. We're proud of what we've accomplished in the past ten years, but we truly feel our best work lies ahead. We've grown from a small magazine for the heads to a force on the newsstand and in music journalism. Revered the world over, connoisseurs are checking for us, and we hope to build on that in the coming decade as we open our pages to a new generation of readers. Like Prince, we'll keep doing us, evolving our steez and staying on top of our game. Two thousand twelve will see more changes, as we slide back into a quarterly schedule and ride out the rest of this recession. These evil streets is rough, so we roll with the rush like Sticky Fingaz. Big shout to our Wax Poetics family all over the globe—from the writers and editors to the artists and advertisers. But most of all, much love to you, our readers, who have been a part of this movement for the past decade and continue to support the cause.

L'Chaim!

Andre Torres, January 2012

"CAN IT BE THAT IT WAS ALL SO SIMPLE THEN?"

–Wu-Tang Clan
"Can It Be All So Simple"

MINNEAPOLIS ROOTS

Grand Central

by **Ericka Blount Danois**

André Cymone and Prince bonded over music in high school and quickly formed a band. From André's parents' basement, André and Prince competitively engaged in all-night jam sessions that would plant the seeds for the funk/rock/pop style that would soon be recognized as "the Minneapolis sound."

In the early 1970s, the Way Community Center, a local recreation center in the heart of Black Minneapolis, hosted battles of the bands as competitive as New York's 1980s rap battles. Flyte Tyme (whose name was inspired by the Charlie Parker recording "Bird in Flight") and Grand Central (inspired by Prince's fascination with Grand Funk Railroad) were two of the most electrifying rival bands.

Considered to be the creation of bassist André Cymone (originally Anderson), Grand Central included André's younger sister, Linda, on keyboards, Terry Jackson and William Doughty on percussion, and drummer Charles "Chazz" Smith (who played football with Terry Lewis in high school and was Prince's cousin), later replaced by a left-handed drummer named Morris Day. The final and most notable member was Prince, plucking the guitar—along with any and all other instruments—with abandon. All of the members ranged in age from thirteen to sixteen and were self-taught musicians. Bernadette, André's mother, a recent divorcée and mother of six children, let them use her basement as their rehearsal space. Prince was also living in the basement after running away from home when he was twelve years

old because of disputes with his stepfather.

"You know how there's one house in the neighborhood that everybody kind of comes to and hangs out? That was my crib," André said in a 1998 interview where he doesn't dispel rumors that it was also a space where they frequently entertained girls.

Their rivals, Flyte Time, included Jimmy Jam, Terry Lewis, Jellybean Johnson, Monte Moir, and Cynthia Johnson. Members of both bands lived within a three-block radius of each other. At Central High School, Jim Hamilton, a former piano player in Ray Charles's band, taught a class about the music business. The same faces appeared in his class—André Anderson, Terry Lewis, William Doughty, and Prince became his mentees. LaVonne Daughtery, Morris Day's mother, became Grand Central's manager.

Grand Central was focused—the group would spend half their days in school and the other half skipping school to rehearse in the basement. They played community centers, YMCAs, and hotels in the area. Flyte Time was more R&B-focused, playing covers of legends like Chaka Khan, Al Green, and James Brown, while Grand Central would play covers from groups ranging from Steely Dan to Sly and the Family Stone.

Pepé Willie, a Brooklyn-born musician with a band of his own named 94 East, would be instrumental in Prince and André's later success. When Pepé first heard Grand Central at a ski party, he asked Daughtery if he could manage the group. He took them to meet Dale Minton, owner of Cookhouse Studios on Nicollett Avenue, armed with a demo of songs like "You Remind Me," "39th Street Party," and "Sex Machine," written by André and Prince.

"He felt they weren't ready," Pepé remembers. "because they would play cover songs better than they would play their own songs. They couldn't show what they could

do on their own."

But they were not without talent. Prince and André stood out from the group.

"Prince would take off his guitar and go over to Linda and play the chords on the keyboard he wanted her to play," Pepé recalls. "And I'm like, 'Wait a minute, this guy plays keyboards too?' Then he would take André's bass and play like he had been doing it for twenty years, playing the funkiest lines. And then André would pick up whatever he wanted him to play like he had been playing it forever. That's how talented these guys were. I was like, 'We got something here.'"

André and Prince would have contests about how fast they could write songs.

"I would say, 'Let's take five,' and we'd go to the kitchen to make some chocolate cake," remembers Pepé. "Prince would stay and wouldn't eat; he would just continue playing. His work ethic started at a real early age."

But André's band was short-lived. They had one last name change to Champagne—when people began comparing them to Graham Central Station—before the group began to disband. Pepé took André under his wing as bassist for 94 East with Colonel Abrams as a vocalist and Bobby Z as a drummer, and they recorded two songs for Polydor—"Fortune Seller" and "10:15"—but, because of problems with the label, their contract was canceled and the songs weren't completed.

Meanwhile, Prince had his sights set on getting out of Minneapolis, and when he met producer Chris Moon and a young manager named Owen Husney, it was the beginning of the end for Grand Central.

"Chris plays me this demo he had been recording on this eight-track," Husney recalls. "Incredible. I was like, 'Who's the group?' And he was like, 'It's not a group. It's one kid, and he's writing and singing and

(*below*) Grand Central. (left to right)
Linda Anderson, André (Cymone)
Anderson, Morris Day, Terry Jackson,
Prince, and William Doughty.
Photographer unknown.

playing everything. I said, 'Holy shit! Get him here now!' "

In a 1982 interview with Nat Morris on Detroit TV show *The Scene*, André didn't mince words when describing Grand Central's band as *his* group. "Morris and Prince was in it," he said matter-of-factly. After the crowd erupted in applause, André smiled and said, "You hear that straight from the horse's mouth."

Prince would go on to define the Minneapolis sound, but André Cymone had a less-celebrated impact. In an interview in *Billboard* magazine, Husney described how Prince and André would stay up all night working on what would eventually become Prince's 1980 album, *Dirty Mind*. Eventually, André became frustrated with his lack of recognition for his contributions and, in 1981, began a solo career with futuristic electronics and signed to Columbia Records, releasing *Livin' in the New Wave* (1982), *Survivin' in the '80s* (1983), and *A.C.* (1985).

"They spent millions of hours jamming together in that basement," says Husney about the group Grand Central. "André had a lot of input into that sound." ◗

33 REASONS
Why Prince Is Hip-Hop

by **Ahmir "Questlove" Thompson**
illustrations by **Josh Dunn**

Questlove is a drummer, a tweeter, a political provocateur, a music encyclopedia, a founding member of hip-hop royalty the Roots, the bandleader of *Late Night with Jimmy Fallon*, and a Prince fanatic. Take a journey through his mind as he argues thirty-three reasons why Prince is "hip-hop."

October 1991 marked the year of a new Prince. I could tell that something was on his mind (perhaps money?). It was his thirteenth professional year, and something had to give. Clearly he was irked by longtime fans already giving his 1978–'88 tenure a past-tense reference (known as "the genius period," similar to pre–*Woman in Red* Stevie's 1971–'76 era, but Prince fared a lil better). Although a commercial success, his 1989 *Batman* soundtrack felt unthawed. (And let's face it: *anything* with that Batlogo was getting copped back in the late '80s, so it was a no-brainer. You could turn in just about anything and it would sell as long as that golden logo was attached to your product.) His next album was a heartbreaking failure of a sequel to the very breakthrough that probably is responsible for this tribute issue you now hold in your hands. *Graffiti Bridge*, released in 1990, did the *exact* opposite of what *Purple Rain* was to do for his career (and it's noted that all of the

soundtrack highlights were indeed written or recorded...during the—*ahem*—"genius period.") However, on Prince and the New Power Generation's *Diamonds and Pearls*, his first "proper" album since 1988's puzzling *Lovesexy* and his first project *not* to reach the top ten since 1981's *Controversy*, Prince seemed to embrace "rap" (not hip-hop, but "rap") almost with the believability of Republican politicians that visit the inner-city slums to kiss babies and shake hands. The puzzling thing about it all is that Prince was more "hip-hop" than he ever was once he gave in to "rap" music.

Dare I say he was a hip-hop pioneer? Yes. *That* Prince. Without even trying, he did things that those in the hip-hop generation wouldn't even think to do some years later in their careers. So in celebration of Prince reaching Jesus status (thirty-three years in the game), I'd like to argue thirty-three reasons why sucker MCs should call him sire.

33 "2 Live, 2 Live is what we are."
In 1988, Prince poses stark naked on his tenth album cover, *Lovesexy*.

32 & 31 "So either join the crew or get beat down."
With Hammer as America's newly discovered go-to guy, Prince reverses his Sir Nose D'VoidoRAP position of the past (more on that later) and full-on puts his career survival ahead of his personal creativity. Backtracking a hard stance, of course, would be the norm come 1997 with the all-integrity no-sell-out hip-hop. Of course, with the formation of the NPG and its kickoff album, 1991's *Diamonds and Pearls*, with samples and rap breaks over a band soundtrack (I'll just sneak in #31 here) and the occasional "nigga" sprinkled for effect (let's not forget the mic gun either), Prince was actually onto something that was years ahead of my own entry in the game.

30 "I got it from my pops, where there's a man in the house and all the bullshit stops."
Genius starts with the act of defiance, achieving something when you are told that you can't achieve. Prince's father told him flat out, "Don't touch my piano." So, naturally, Prince takes that to mean, "Please help yourself, then help me some twenty years later by taking care of me with the fruits of your labor." I don't know if the Joseph/Tito thing went down, but I do know that he taught himself to play the theme to *Batman* (See? The man is a visionary!) and soon he got more intricate—that is, until he got kicked out the house and shuffled around to various relatives until running away at the age of twelve.

29 "Check it, fifteen of us in a three-bedroom apartment.
Roaches everywhere, cousins and aunts was there.
Four in a bed, two at the foot, two at the head."
The Anderson family basement. P's BFF André Anderson (aka Cymone) asks his mom, Bernadette, to take in "Skipper" as her seventh child. She does so, and also puts up with all the noise, knowing it's better to be inconvenienced than those two to be running out in the streets.

28 "Shakespeare couldn't tell a story that well."
Prince's bio stretched the truth quite a bit. Shaved his age a little bit to grab teen market. Embellished his ability. (Don't get me wrong, he can play anything he wants to, but if you list over twenty instruments, and fifteen of those instruments are keyboard related, then, yeah, it's impressive to someone who don't know any better; but in my head, you play three instruments: drums, bass, and guitar. Okay, I'll be fair and say four—and keyboards. Not: (1) Organ—no organ on his first seven records! (2) Rhodes (3) Clavinet (4) Synth. (5) Piano... Come on, now.) Now, the previously mentioned coulda been record-label politics. But in early interviews (especially with *Right On!* teen mag), Prince too was having some fun making up his bio on the spot to get some hood cred. My favorite being how he was so poor, he'd steal Bubble Yum and stand in front of a McDonald's just to pretend he was eating a meal.

27, 26, & 25 "The shoes (the shoes?)… It's gotta be the shoes!"

Unusual footwear is the most definitive rebel statement one can make in hip-hop. Some take the strings out, some rock mismatched, and with a better budget, some can rock just about anything. But it takes a true man to rock heels with confidence. Hip-hop can posture all it wants, but to get yo chick stolen from a dude looking like him is a hurt piece. (Let's not forget #26, feathering his hair in '79 and '88–'90, and #25, his Black-hippy period of '85–'87, having heavy influence on West Coast rappers and the Native Tongues, respectively.)

24 "Who put this thing together, huh? Me! Me, that's who!! Who I trust? Who I trust? *Me*!"

Prince Rogers Nelson aka Jamie Starr aka Alexander Nevermind aka Joey Cocoa aka Camille aka Victor aka the Kid aka Christopher Tracey aka TAFKAP aka "Taffy" aka Tora Tora aka Violet the Organ-grinder aka Gemini aka Ecnirp aka NPG2000 aka the Artist aka Paisley Park aka Skipper aka His Royal Badness aka Azifwekare aka the Wise One aka…Prince? (Wonder what his Wu-Tang name would be?)

23 "This is a gang, and I'm in it!"

Rule number one in any musical success is the idea of community. He who walks alone, starves alone (except novelty one-hit wonders). Check the books: Motown (Diana, Marvin, Tempts, Smokey, Stevie), British invasion (Stones, Beatles, Kinks, Who, Cream); Native Tongues (De La, Tribe, Jungle, Latifah, Black Sheep, Monie); Young Money (Wayne, Drake, Nick). Or if you in a class by yourself, you can pull the tricky dim sum method. (Jay-Z is a *master* of this: Bad Boy, Roots, Good Music, Young Money, State Property, and whoever is buzzed about, he is *on* it!) So Prince wisely saw that he needed too much posse to not only nuance his perceived weirdness, but to pretty much build an empire: the Time was his Black side, Vanity/Ap 6 was his female side, Sheila was his Latin-jazz virtuoso side, the Family was his '80s pop side, Madhouse was his jazz side, and NPG was…well.

22 "So sit and analyze the lyrical spray, 'cause all it really is is wordplay."

Funny how a song like "Sister" has you questioning what he really means when he is clearly spelling it out. But "Little Red Corvette," "Tambourine," "The Stick," and "Sugar Walls," with all its hidden entendres, were obvious as hell to my authority figures.

21 & 20 "Backseat of my Jeep, let's swing an episode."

What self-respecting pimp would pass up a shot inside the ride? (A ride he loves so much, he declares to trash all his worldly possessions for the love of his life, only to renege on "the ride," which in itself is #20.) But what I find the most interesting is, like a lot of pre-1997 hip-hop, why is Prince, a full-on adult (he himself said sixteen is half a man—so being that he was twenty-two when "Dirty Mind" came out…), still living with his parents?

19 "I was gettin' some, get gettin' some…"

Capn' Save-a-Bride fails Pimping 101 by marrying his one-night stand (or one-day stand, wedding day, at that) by "Head"'s last verse. Wonder if Lisa Coleman got her one-take Hov on with "You're such a hunk" without breaking character?

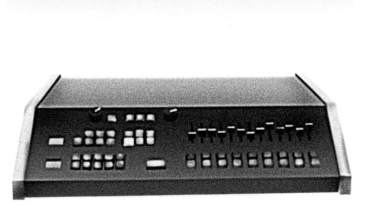

18 "I got a letter from the government the other day, I opened and read it..." Prince's war paranoia ("Partyup," "Free," "Ronnie Talk to Russia," even "After Hi-School" for the Time) was an occasional head-scratcher. But not as hardly head-scratching as his other steeze.

17 "Illuminati got my mind, soul, and my body." The end times had Money *'noid.* Word is bond, son. His peerless musicianship (more later) distracted me from the fact that his pop breakthrough, "1999," was some conspiracy theory jib-jab about how after 2000, people are just gonna roam the earth bombing *ish*, and how nobody was gonna be safe anymore. Psssh, just shut up and play yer guitar, ya crazy person, you. "Mommy, why does everybody have a–*KABLAMO*!!!!!!" Ha! That's just crazy talk, young man.

16 "Now there's this thing called the drum machine, you don't need good rhythm to sound real mean." Prince's greatest gift to hip-hop (and most post–civil rights R&B) was his peerless and boundless ability to program and mix drum machines. He used his guitar effects to get new sounds out of them. He often substituted sounds for others (high-pitched tambourine was hi-hat, snare rim shot were congas, lowered cowbells were tom-toms). Not to mention, the actual programming was done so precise you too thought it was done by a human (not even gonna speak on spending three months in 1982 tryna master "777-9311" to find out it was a machine). But while we're on the subject of giving the drummer some, let's not sleep on #15.

15 "Stuffs and thangs to make the people git outcha seat." In my opinion, *Parade*, with its orchestral patches, jazz structure, and sloppy post–"Mother's Son" (google that Curtis classic) funk drumming, birthed Dilla's neo-soul movement. Which left me kinda weirded-out when his "neo-soul" offering (*The Rainbow Children*) sounded like a copy of the artists who were copying him ten years before. And since we're on jazz…

14 "The jazz, the what, the jazz to move that ass." Seen as jazz albums, I could understand the need for him to get all shy about promoting Madhouse *8* and *16* in case real jazz musicians wanted to come at his neck for faking it (for the record, I love these records!). However, seen in a hip-hop context, Madhouse was some progressive funk and the closest thing to a breakbeat-mentality fusion approach that *any* jazz dude ever attempted in some organic manner. (Yes, Herb/Laswell included.) There were breaks and loops galore for the taking. No complaints here.

13 **"Get you bling like the Neptunes sound."**
Although the post-'98 minimalist Swiss/'Tunes entry of hip-hop at first appeared to be complete lazy, half-baked opposite of the hard work laid down by the "fill up all the spacisms" of the Bomb Squad/Dust Brothers sound collage that came before it, in reality, the birth of keyboard beats can be traced to a lil ditty called "When Doves Cry," a song so controversial for its omittance of the bass that when it first came out, cats just knew that a coalition fronted by Clarke/Johnson/Graham/Brunson would form a lynch mob out of anger.

12 **"Ghostwriter, and for the right price, I can even make yo shit tighter."**
I never completely got the "market this guy as genius, but then shroud him in mystery when it's so clearly him." He even went as far as to call his own id (Jamie Starr) a thief on "DMSR." It's like, "Come on, dude, we so know it's you writing this stuff." Not to mention, he singlehandedly invented ghetto shorthand with all of his trademark shortcut spellings. Man, my teachers were relieved when I dropped that habit, I tell ya.

11 **"Introducing the world's most controversial dangerous label."**
Vanity labels are nothing in today's hip-hop environment. But back in the '80s, it was a rarity. Borderline nonexistent. There was no Lionel's Hello Records or Rick's Punk Funk Label or Michael's Menagerie. Of course, vanity labels are nothing but production companies with elaborate artwork. It's just a shame P wasn't able to establish his Paisley Park brand back in '81 when his Starr-making purple wand was nothing but net.

10 **"I got somethin' to say, 'Fuck tha police!' "**
He taunted them in "DMSR." He fingers them in the Time's "The Walk." He even, uh, fingers himself while getting caught by them in New York. But make no mistake, no hip-hop pioneer got love for jake.

9 **"I used to sell mixtapes, but now I'm an MC."**
Prince is hands down *thee* most bootlegged artist in the modern rock era, with over three hundred unreleased songs, rehearsals, and concerts being traded like rare baseball cards. The most famous of these taboo recordings was a lil side project that was part "party music" to be used for a pal's birthday party (the pal being Sheila E.) and part response to purists who accused him of forgetting where he came from (which is weird, 'cause I don't think ghetto streets when I think of the Twin Cities). But anyhoo, before its five-years-too-late official release in '94 (contractual obligations), the myth of *The Black Album* spawned an insatiable appetite for Prince fans to obtain even more unavailable material as it came down the pike. He, of course, despises the thought of millions he coulda made, but all it did was reaffirm and solidify his genius. (And since we're on the subject, let's segue into #8.)

POLICE DEPT.
JACKSON, MISS
20897
3-2980

8 "Tryin to rap up, but you can't get down.
You don't even know your English, your verb, or nouns.
You're just a sucker MC, you sad-face clown."
Of course, hating on other MCs is a natural thing in hip-hop. It's just head-scratching that his disdain for rap prompted a response that was rapped, which also marked the first time he flirts with making bad rap songs. Which was a shame considering (as said before), he was more "hip-hop" not even knowing he was hip-hop.

"Dead On It" is his only misstep of the legendary underground classic *The Black Album*.

7 "And fuck Tommy Boy, 'cause them niggas just suck."
As long as Prince was living and fulfilling his potential, there seemed to be no beef with Warner Bros. He demanded no outside producers, and they let him. He demanded a production development deal, and they let him. He demanded to make a movie, and they let him. He went far left and they let him. He made a bummer of a second film, and they let him. He made whatever music he wanted to, and they let him. He posed nude on his album cover, and they let him. He took a single to *another* label, and they let him. And when he couldn't take it no more, his last words on his last album for them were "Fuck You!"

6 "We invented the remix."
The whole idea of reinventing yourself and your song really starts with him. I was cool with "Little Red Corvette," but if you'd told me, "I just heard that on the radio, and it's Prince's funkiest jam," I woulda looked at you like you were crazy. But sure enough, Prince turned his rockiest song into a eight-minute funk workout as if we never heard the original. Before him, "remixes" were just edits, cuts, and pasting. With him, you now have the chance to make your jam appeal to a broader (and sometimes Blacker) demographic.

5 "Banned in the USA."
First Lady hopeful starts a movement to protect young America from the filthy vile minds from the likes of… Prince? PMRC insists on Parental Advisory stickers for records thanks to sex fiends and their magazines.

4 **"When I see you, guaranteed to be an ICU."**
No true hip-hop pioneer is universally loved. But they are respected. P being no exception. He (allegedly) done stole Rick James's honey (Vanity in '79 backstage at the AMAs), he done stole Rick's potential money (the 1980 *Fire It Up* tour has a crazy legend that the opening act from Minniap would clear the house before the headline came on), his dreams (Rick too had Hollywood movies in his eye as a breakthrough for a bigger audience), his ideas (Vanity 6 vs. the Mary Jane Girls), even his background singers (longtime Prince associate Jill Jones first met him as background singer for *Fire It Up* tour act Teena Marie), and, according to Rick, everything else. Rick was relentless in publicly airing out why he couldn't stand that "yella midget." Who do you think let the cat out the bag about Charlie Murphy getting his arse waxed in b-ball? That was unforgivable in Rick's eyes.

3 **"You was a Reebok vandal, now you wear Chanel sandals.**
I made you, why would I play you?"
I mean, it's redundant to even state, but the exotic laced-up beauty there on your arm (or your screensaver?), Prince singlehandedly invented that. Real talk.

2 **"I just wanna tape you. All night. Yeah!"**
Misunderstood, under-six-foot artist from the Midwest with dreams of making it big who doesn't look the part of the music he performs. His fellow peers are rivals that will spare no expense in trying to embarrass him. Gets a pretty girl, but loses a pretty girl to a rival. Lives at home with parents; got beef with parents. Someone gets shot. The world is closing in. Music saves him. Has to battle in club to save rep. End result is an Oscar. The world is even in more love with him. I'm talking about *8 Mile*, what were you thinking about?

1 **"I'm every MC. It's all in me."**
Accused others of bitin', runs ball, always had a brand-new dance up his sleeve, borrowed from James Brown, had a "Blackman is God" moment personifying himself as Jesus, made album skits, made nine-minute songs sometimes, made fun of hipsters ("We don't like new wave"), but adapted the hipster mantra of "Thou must hate TV," used gunplay, "Nigger" in song title, used songs for bait for supermodels, hopped label to label, sampled himself, sampled others, had sex on wax, took someone's virginity, sang of his virginity getting…uh…taken at sixteen, sang about NYC, sang about critics, sang of future technology, blamed women for his problems, had good vs. evil conflicts, looked for the *ladder* first, got booed and pelted with chicken bones, sang of paranoia, had cab troubles, addressed the president, writing his name in graffiti on the wall, chased 'em, replaced 'em, and leave without a traced 'em. And most importantly, came to this Earth with more a title than name.

Prince. ⊙

ESCAP ISM
Blood Orange

by **David Ma**

Blood Orange is the newest moniker of prolific producer and multi-instrumentalist Devonté Hynes. After making a mark with the garage band Test Icicles and his folk alter ego Lightspeed Champion, Hynes has finally hit his groove, crafting a hallucinatory, yet highly personal, glimpse of the future of R&B.

In tight, ripped jeans, glasses, tank top, and backwards cap, Devonté Hynes records as Blood Orange, a recent handle for the twenty-five-year-old musician. His solo sets are minimal; he croons and shreds guitar while triggering sounds from his laptop. And for years, out of necessity and preference, lonely bars were his main practice space. "I literally had nowhere to just mess around, be loud, and play. I lived in small apartments, and the only time I could do whatever was on weeknights in random spots somewhere," he remembers, laughing. "It's funny, my friends say I'm the guy who won't tell anyone about his gigs. [*laughs*] I'd just book a show and come alone to play. But, *really*, it was the only way I could practice, and I'm grateful I was able to take advantage of it." Playing for slow-sippers indifferent to live music gave him room to breathe, to freely play without having to align or explain himself to anyone.

Dev's persona isn't entirely easy to depict. His musical training began early, but his inspirations are quite varied. "I started playing piano at seven, moving onto the cello, then drums, then bass; everything just fell around that. I don't know what else to say," he says, rather apologetically. In his mid-twenties, he's young and has had lifelong musical training. He avoids the spotlight but moves easily beneath it. His favorites are completely wide-ranging, so much so, it's difficult to tell what and who has bled into his work. He cites

(*previous spread and right*)
Devonté Hynes aka Blood Orange.
Photos by Shawn Brackbill.

The vocals, soft and breathy, have been likened to Prince, an aforementioned favorite of Dev's. "On face value, that's an amazing compliment but also a million miles off the mark," he laughs. "*Who* could ever truly be compared to Prince?"

Janet Jackson, Pantera, Marilyn Manson, and Prince as leaving huge imprints—as did Arthur Russell, Phillip Glass, and Ryuichi Sakamoto of Yellow Magic Orchestra. He says further: "I could also recite the words to, like, every rap song while growing up." Adding: "Oh yeah, and Marvin Gaye is one of the best singers *ever*."

He's foggy, scattered almost, when explaining his influences but speaks easily on finding strength in transgender culture and its history. Admittedly, all his new songs are written "from a female perspective," he says. The inspiration derived from transgender and gay history is perhaps linked to his own dealings with intolerance. "I felt a lot prejudice growing up—*a lot*," he reiterates. "Even though I'm not gay, I felt a lot of gay prejudice and homophobia from kids because of what I wore and what I was into. I mean, I played football when I was young, and I absolutely love the NBA. But I also played cello and was in the chess club. [*laughs*] Where I'm from, I guess I always stuck out for all sorts of reasons."

Originally born in Houston, Texas, Dev and his family relocated early on to Essex, a non-metropolitan area in Eastern England where most of his childhood was spent. He left for the big city of London as a teenager, continuing all the way to Los Angeles. His wanderlust led him to Queens, New York, around 2006. He now lives in Brooklyn where *Coastal Grooves*, his newest, most distinct work, developed gradually in his bedroom through the last few years. Like most young musicians, Dev was in many bands with assorted styles, lobbing darts and seeing which ones stuck.

His first troupe, Test Icicles, made spastic rock with overtly thrashy sounds. It was a learning experience in working with others, says Dev. "We would all write by ourselves and come in the studio and record, then have someone come in and overdub certain parts and segments. People were in and out all the time. We would record, and rerecord, and rerecord. I know that's normal, but it wasn't my style. Sometimes it went well, sometimes it was absolutely painstaking." The band released one official project before disbanding in 2006.

Moving away from group dynamics, Dev forged Lightspeed Champion, a more subdued, folk-driven solo effort with clangy guitars, handclaps, and pop melodies—much different from the raucous noise of Test Icicles. Reasonable success was had in both ventures; units sold moderately well and album reviews were pleasant. But it was Dev's songwriting prowess that heads picked up on, asking him eventually to write for their own acts. His writing acumen gave him work for a diverse cast, a reflection perhaps of the range easily seen in his own songs. He quietly penned for a hodgepodge of artists: Basement Jaxx, Florence and the Machine (whose album hit number one on the U.K. music charts), and musical sketches for television's *Saturday Night Live*. He also contributed to the Chemical Brothers' *We Are the Night*, a hit Grammy winner that same year. He meanwhile scattered songs and compositions on the Internet via blogs and message boards on his own as well.

With projects on the upswing, Dev returned to recording by himself and for himself, explaining: "I'd write in the kitchen,

record in the bedroom, and randomly play out all by myself." He even reverted to playing small bars for practice, basking in the anonymity, especially since it was purely practice nevertheless. "There's no pressure whatsoever, and people generally don't know what to expect when they see me," he says, adding: "I still wouldn't tell anyone I was playing, because I wanted to be alone and just practice stuff I felt I liked. It was just some songs I started during [and a little after] the last Lightspeed Champion album. I was still trying things out—they weren't even whole recordings yet." These songs, essentially ideas and rough sketches, became the template for Blood Orange.

Around 2008, however, a persistent aching developed in Dev's throat, leading to emergency surgery that put his career—and worse possibly, his voice—in jeopardy. Diagnosed with growths on his vocal chords, called nodules, it was unclear if he'd ever sing again, or sound as he did before surgery. It's thought to have developed from overworking his voice through constant gigging, a condition that affected Elton John and other notable—but mostly longtime—vocalists. And while severity of the condition greatly varies, it was nonetheless a sobering time. Dev recalls, "I had to have them removed, and doctors didn't even know exactly how it would alter my voice. It was pretty weird and scary but was fun sometimes too. [laughs] Overall, I couldn't speak at all for two months and basically had to learn how to sing all over again. I'm so grateful it worked out; but at first, it was like running into a brick wall."

With speech therapy that followed, Dev regained speech function and recovered while reworking the Blood Orange sketches that had sat dormant on his hard drive. He eventually ironed out enough tracks for a demo, an EP that he slid to friends and label affiliates. "They were just short bits of songs I'd listen to when I was on my skateboard or riding around the city on my bike. I didn't play them to anyone, and I came to realize that for the first time ever, really, I was trying to write the kind of songs I actually wanted to hear."

The demo made its rounds and was well received, especially since insiders were acquainted with his writing credits. The EP was eventually picked up by Domino Records,

an indie label based in the U.K. The imprint wanted a longer, more fully realized project, and newer songs were added to flesh out the release; existing songs were rerecorded professionally in the studio.

The resulting *Coastal Grooves* is Dev's debut, or rather, his newest incarnation as Blood Orange, a deviation from his existing works. The album has nods to new wave and R&B but also has the drive of '80s power pop. Aesthetically, Asian melodies and timbres push up-tempo drums along with synth sounds. "I used my guitar, bass, keyboard, and laptop, and just basically put everything together at home," he says of the album, which has predominately been labeled as indie-dance rock. But there are strong currents of disco and David Bowie throughout; a bit of Cyndi Lauper and Bohannon too. The vocals, soft and breathy, have been likened to Prince, an aforementioned favorite of Dev's. "On face value, that's an amazing compliment but also a million miles off the mark," he laughs, adding to it: "*Who* could ever truly be compared to Prince? It's mainly just a comparison to what he did on *Purple Rain*, not the million other records he made. I'm sure he'd be offended at the thought of my shitty plug-ins and Garage Band bullshit being compared to his production," he says, laughing.

There is a sense of androgyny found on *Coastal Grooves* that merits some of the Prince talk, a fact Dev concedes to. Actually, it's his new outlook that's entirely bolstered his approach to songwriting. "I love androgyny in music—in general, I love androgyny. But somewhere along the way, the lines got blurred. I'm at a point now where every song I write, it just comes natural for me to think and sound androgynous. It's a girlish register I've worked really hard at [in order] for it to sound properly when doing it. I probably did it most on this Blood Orange album." He continues, "It's all about *escapism*, about running away, and the idea of freedom. I guess the only real main inspiration was Octavia."

Octavia St. Laurent was a transgender model from 1980s New York and was featured prominently in the revered film *Paris Is Burning*. The documentary examined gay Harlem and New York City "drag balls." It was a subculture comprised primarily of transgender and gay men, most of them Latin and African American. "[St. Laurent] died

two years ago from cancer and HIV-related causes. I was thinking about her the whole time while making *Coastal Grooves*. Just the basic idea of having a place to go hide, to feel comfortable, and just really be oneself spoke to me. You can see it in the film, and she really lived her life that way."

The artwork for *Coastal Grooves* also affirms its sexual and emotional themes—a drag queen adorns the cover, posing in front of Sally's Hideaway, a well-known nightclub that existed in Times Square between 1986 and 1992. It was a mecca for gay and transgender men and a fixture of the 1980s gay-power movement. The picture was taken by Brian Lance, a photographer who was also a part of *Paris Is Burning*. Dev selected the cover art after a chance meeting with Lance. "I made contact with Brian through the Internet while I was googling Octavia and found all these wonderful photos he took during that era." Some of those images are now part of *Coastal Grooves'* overall design aesthetic and media campaign. "I'm sure some people will see it and not know what to make if it," says Dev. "But to me, it was the perfect fit. It's probably the one thing the record directly relates to."

Dev recently embarked on his first solo tour as Blood Orange, having just written and produced for Theophilus London's newest project. He is also working with Beyoncé's younger sibling, Solange Knowles, on her upcoming project. Through all the fogginess, it's clear that Dev is a young artist whose career is in the ascendant—his next album could be a complete deviation from what he's into at the moment of this writing. But he's untrammeled by notions of sexuality and style, an outlook that seemingly—and refreshingly—underpins all his work regardless of genre.

"I was already in New York at the time and kept thinking about how difficult being Black must've been in the '80s. Then I thought about how harder it must've been being Black *and* gay! But some people were, are, Black, gay, *and* transgender! How I was then, how I am now, basically, was always different for whatever reason. I *get* that feeling, and that's what shows most on this record, on this whole Blood Orange thing, I think. There's a lot of people running away in these songs." ⬤

SY NCOP ATE D STRUT

Madhouse

by **Miles Marshall Lewis**

Prince and reed man Eric Leeds teamed up to create two albums under the moniker Madhouse. Perhaps looking to exorcise jazz demons inherited from his father, Prince masterminded a lighthearted and funky sound that anticipated the "acid jazz" genre that would break years later.

The DJ at Le Réservoir spins nothing but 1980s vinyl loaded with LinnDrum beats and synthesizers for Parisians packing the smallish dance floor, but nobody minds. The NPG Party is the only fête in town where gorgeous French women gladly fall into step with the mechanized drum programming on Sheila E. rare grooves like "Too Sexy" and "Shortberry Strawcake." The infectious blend of funk-rock, new wave, and R&B music once known as the Minneapolis Sound prepares everyone for tonight's main event: Rad, featuring saxophonist Eric Leeds.

You see, Rad is an alumna of the New Power Generation, class of 2004. And Leeds famously spent years in the Revolution during the mid-'80s. Both groups have flanked Prince, architect of the Minneapolis Sound, stretching back over two decades. So Rad—born Rose Ann Dimalanta—will be preaching to the converted this springtime Sunday night.

Rad, a petite forty-year-old Filipina in a sleeveless sequined top with white slacks, stands center stage behind her bank of synths at the stroke of nine. Fronting a five-piece band, she powers through many original funk numbers from her own records for over an hour before dipping into the catalog of the man whose genius has been the purple elephant in the room through her whole show.

"Mutiny! I said I'm taking over," Rad sings, atop James Brownish staccato horn blasts from Eric Leeds. "You gotta give up this ship. You should've been a little more hip."

Tall, lanky, and bespectacled, suited in all black, fifty-seven-year-old Leeds eyes trombonist Greg Boyer (another NPG alum) as a quick signal before blowing the house down. Leeds approximates his own original solo from "Mutiny," recorded back in late 1984 for the eponymously titled album of Prince protégé band the Family.

Known intimately by the dancing crowd at Le Réservoir, the Family is most familiar to the general public for "Nothing Compares 2 U," a ballad brought to the top of worldwide charts by Sinéad O'Connor in 1990. Nominally an R&B quintet, the Family stands tall in Prince lore for introducing live horns into the one-man band's musical output. *The Family* secretly features Prince undercover on every instrument except Eric Leeds's saxophone and flute. The group was predictably short-lived, but not before inspiring Prince to create another pseudo band with himself secretly playing every instrument except Leeds's sax and flute.

That band was the jazz-fusion outfit Madhouse. Drummer Billy Johnson strikes the opening fill to "Six," and the crowd goes wild. At the lip of the stage, a dredlocked fan starts acting out with a French brunette, throwing up goofy Egyptian hieroglyphic hand gestures and shimmying around. Because if you paid twenty-five euros to see Eric Leeds play an intimate Parisian nightclub, Madhouse's "Six" is the song you've been waiting all night long to hear. Sax and keyboard variations on one sinuous musical riff center "Six" in a funky, rhythmic groove; "Six" reached number five on *Billboard*'s Black Singles Chart in early 1987, the age of *Beverly Hills Cop*'s hit instrumental, "Axel F."

Madhouse, for the relatively few paying attention, was one of those riddles wrapped in a mystery inside an enigma that Churchill talked about. Every piece of the group's cover art—two albums, three singles—featured only twenty-one-year-old Maneca Lightner, credited as the "Madhouse cover girl," dressed in sexy

polka-dotted outfits with a Yorkshire terrier. Lightner, it so happens, was dating Prince casually at the time. Warner Bros. Records released the band's first album, *8*, through Prince's Paisley Park Records label on January 21, 1987, and the album credits made no mention of the band members. Those same credits claimed that *8* was recorded at Madhouse Studios in Pittsburgh, a studio that doesn't exist.

The riddle-mystery-enigma went even deeper. Minnesota's *Star Tribune* reviewed *8* the day after its release and presented Madhouse as the brainchild of Atlanta keyboardist Austra Chanel. The group, according to an official bio from publicist Howard Bloom, consisted of Chanel, drummer John Lewis, bassist Bill Lewis, and Eric Leeds. As you might gather by now, neither Chanel nor the Lewis brothers existed either, but nationwide newspapers and magazines began echoing the misinformation.

Warner Bros. delivered Madhouse's *16* album on November 18, just ten months after *8*, with bass player Levi Seacer Jr. and keyboardist Matt Fink added to the lineup, real-life musicians from Prince's recent touring band for his *Sign o' the Times* album. Stranger still, that two-month European tour featured Madhouse as the opening act with a slightly different lineup, essentially the *16* assemblage but with longtime Prince associate Dale Alexander on drums.

Prince was already infamous for this kind of playful deception. By 1987, he was notorious for writing effortless hit singles for others using flimsy pseudonyms. Nobody believed Christopher (of the Bangles' "Manic Monday") or Alexander Nevermind (Sheena Easton's "Sugar Walls") composed anything. Beginning with the Time and continuing with Vanity 6, Apollonia 6, Sheila E., the Family, and Jill Jones, Prince was also legendary for writing and playing most everything on his protégés' records. Madhouse marked the last time in Prince's career that he ever would. (Subsequent Paisley Park acts—the Three O'Clock, Dale Bozzio, Tony LeMans, Taja Sevelle, Good Question, Carmen Electra—were, for better or worse, largely left to their own devices.) Never again would Prince go to such absurd lengths to pretend he had nothing to do with an act he wrote and

played almost everything for.

Fans collect near the soundboard of Le Réservoir after the show, where Rad stands behind a table posing for photos, selling CDs, and autographing them. To the side is Eric Leeds, with his own display of solo albums: his début *Times Squared*, *Things Left Unsaid*, *Now & Again*, *Cleopatra's Dream*. No Madhouse.

You can chase Prince's jazz ambitions and the origins of Madhouse down several avenues. Son of jazz pianist John L. Nelson, Prince was born with improvisation, syncopation, and swing in his blood. His own instrumental compositions date back to "God (Love Theme from *Purple Rain*)," recorded in February '84 and released as the U.K. B-side of "Purple Rain." Two years later, the *Parade* era's slight piano meditation "Venus de Milo" and sublime rock ballad "Alexa de Paris" (B-side of the "Mountains" single) were more excursions into jazz territory, but they arrived a year after two significant Eric Leeds collaborations on *The Family*. "Susannah's Pajamas" and "Yes," also recorded in '84, laid a notable foundation for Madhouse.

Eric Jeffrey Leeds was born on January 19, 1952, into a middle-class family in Milwaukee. His father, Herbert, ran a Gimbels department store and later founded the Leeds Business Counseling retail-consulting firm; his mother, Dorothy, had been a lieutenant in the navy during WWII. At the age of fourteen, his family relocated to Pittsburgh, and Eric began studying under blind saxophone prodigy Eric Kloss.

Signed to Prestige Records, Kloss had previously recorded with famed Miles Davis rhythm section musicians Jack DeJohnette and Chick Corea, among others. Influenced by the hard bop style of Ray Charles saxophonist David "Fathead" Newman, Leeds played funk, R&B, and jazz fusion in Pennsylvania clubs throughout the late '70s and early '80s with a local eight-piece band called Takin' Names.

When Bruce Springsteen kicked off his *Born in the USA* tour from Minnesota in June 1984, the state's premier rock star paid a backstage visit. The meeting with Springsteen and the late E Street Band

saxman Clarence Clemons may have inspired Prince to add live brass to his own band, a theory Leeds once shared with Prince biographer Per Nilsen in *Dance Music Sex Romance: Prince – The First Decade*.

By then, former James Brown tour manager Alan Leeds (Eric's older brother) had started setting dates for the upcoming *Purple Rain* tour, having joined Prince's team a year earlier. Prince expressed his need for a saxophone player; Alan passed along an audition tape Eric had already submitted to Sheila E. to join *her* band that spring. And on November 15, as the *Purple Rain* tour passed through North Carolina, Prince asked the thirty-two-year-old saxophonist onstage with the Revolution for "Baby, I'm a Star." Leeds soon became a fixture on the tour, in just the right place at the right time for the creation of the Family.

"I remember it started with him calling me one afternoon and asking if I would like to come over to his house and 'play some jazz,'" Eric Leeds remembers, reflecting on that fateful Friday. "I think he said his father was there also, though by the time I got there, his father had left. Prince had some tracks already recorded. We sat at the piano and worked out the melody lines, which were mostly his, and the harmonic changes for the solos. Then we went in the studio, and I started playing. We recorded the entire album over the course of three days."

Done from September 28 to October 1, 1986, at the basement studio of Prince's ranch-style mansion on Galpin Boulevard in suburban Chanhassen, Minnesota, Madhouse's *8* was in stores by January '87. Eight instrumental tunes—entitled "One," "Two," "Three," etc.—made up the thirty-eight-minute album. Portuguese eye candy Maneca Lightner adorned the sleeve wearing a two-piece, 1950s-style polka-dotted swimsuit with a red wide-brim sun hat. Picture the buxom Lightner on a beach, hand on her hip, between a sandcastle and a Yorkie begging on its hind legs for the red ball in her other hand. On the jacket's flip side, she lifts her doggie for a kiss. They saved the back shot (you knew there'd be one) for the single, "Six," Miss Lightner standing on the sand with her booty facing

photographer Richard Litt's camera.

"I honestly don't remember, because that was my first time in L.A.," Lightner says now from Los Angeles, trying to remember the location of the shoot. "Most beach areas look alike, and I'm sure they told me back then, but I can't be certain. If I had to guess, I would have to say somewhere in Malibu, but I'm simply not sure." Richard Litt confirms: "The first shooting was in Malibu, and the following day, I shot in a studio in downtown Los Angeles. The dog was rented from an agency."

Imagine the surprise Prince's demo tape stirred up for Warner Bros. execs in the '70s when they realized the teen wonder was rocking every instrument Stevie Wonder style. *8* carries the same shock. Jazz, even the fusion derivative of the mid-'80s, is rooted in improvisation. Jazzman Prince layering his piano and keyboards on top of his own bass, on top of his own drums, continuously reacting to himself as a stranger from a musician's point of view, is Prince earning his musical genius reputation.

"I did all the sax and flute, and Prince played everything else," Eric Leeds confirms. "Much has been said about his insistence on not letting it be known that he was involved with the project. His motives are his own, but as I remember it, he wanted the music to be related to on its own merits, and perhaps was concerned that if it was released as a 'Prince jazz album,' it would draw more attention to the idea that Prince would play jazz than to the value of the music itself.

"The jazz community can be pretty brutal in its regard for the idea that a pop musician would have the arrogance to consider himself a jazz musician. By the 'jazz community,' I mean the writers and critics. Ironically, many jazz musicians that I know really dug the album and were convinced that Prince was behind it from the very start."

Saxophonist James Carter, cause of the greatest buzz in modern jazz since the debut of Pulitzer-winning trumpeter Wynton Marsalis, remembers *8* fondly. "Man, Madhouse brings back memories of a high school talent show in which we performed 'Six' as an instrumental," says

Carter, recalling his Northwestern High days in Detroit. "I always dug Eric Leeds's sparse baritone sax work throughout the piece. Prince lays down one of the funkiest grooves in D minor; Eric jabs like a boxer."

You could visit certain hipsters in 1965 and be guaranteed to find John Coltrane's *A Love Supreme* in their living rooms. Fast-forward to '73 and we're talking *Head Hunters* by Herbie Hancock. Aside from being landmark albums in jazz, the records were badges of cool for their time (and even now), tchotchkes that revealed as much about the buyers' sophistication as their tastes in music. Believe it or not, *8* became one of those records in 1987.

The album *8* didn't even go gold (marking 500,000 copies in sales). Anyone owning a copy in the late '80s was either (1) a Paisley Park fanatic, or (2) a young somebody searching for an entrée into contemporary jazz, introduced to Madhouse by a diehard Prince lover. Even now, mere mention of Madhouse's *8* works as a password into a Skull and Bones–like secret society, separating true Prince followers from the wannabes.

For a jazz album without any vocals, *8* is a vividly describable record. For starters, Prince is a sexy beast on the drums. These aren't his trusty LinnDrum beats; these are all-the-way-live crash and splash cymbals, toms, bass, snare, and hi-hat drums. But it's the little idiosyncrasies that turn *8* into a charming, descriptive record. The Beatlesesque quirks in his music were always equally as responsible for Prince's cult following as the music itself: backwards guitar solos, hidden messages revealed by spinning the vinyl counterclockwise, self-referential in-jokes. *8* contains enough of these eccentricities to keep things patently Prince.

"Two," for instance, is a mid-tempo number (no pun intended) that slowly builds up to a climactic keyboard solo. But the entire song runs over a comical conversation you can never quite hear clearly. "My theory behind playing the saxophone is very easy," someone says at the beginning. "Blow in one end." Later on, the same joker questions, "Can I get sued for plagiarism? Everybody shut up and listen to me. Where's the melody?" You have to strain to hear punch lines like, "That's why

I get paid by the note," until the tune ends gently with the delayed *tsss* of a cymbal. What the hell were they talking about? We'll never know.

A series of eleven phone-conversation samples runs through "Five." Prince starts a leisurely funky drum pattern that builds in speed and gets measured out by drum-machine handclaps. Meanwhile, snatches of "Five Star Restaurant, can I help you?," "Hi, Mom, this is Jimbo," and "How ya doin', sexy?" keep floating by, sometimes accelerated Kanye West–style, sometimes slowed to a drawl. In less than two minutes, the drums hurtle to a climax and the song finishes with the loud voice of an irate dad: "Hello, son, what took you so long to call?"

Then there's the orgasm. "Six" segues into "Seven" with some uncredited ecstasy from Vanity, a snippet from the unreleased, heavily bootlegged Vanity 6 gem, "Vibrator." Loading her body massager full of (ten!) fresh batteries, Vanity pleasures herself for nearly two minutes at the song's close; Prince cuts and pastes some of her peaking at the end of *8*'s "Four," and as the transition from "Six" into "Seven." (He used it again years later for the *Come* track, "Orgasm.")

"Eight" begins with the repetitive, electronically altered voice of Prince saying what sounds like "hum" over soothing synthesizer atmospherics and flute from Eric Leeds. The title track builds for about eight minutes with saxophone and keyboard solos, until finally ending with two minutes of calm, Brian Eno–like ambient chords. Prince later lifted the closing emotional tones of "Eight" for the introduction to "U Got the Look" that December. Warner Bros. released *Sign o' the Times* two months after *8*, making the "U Got the Look" opening recognizable right away to ardent fans, another of his in-the-know nudge-winks.

The *16* album took shape as Madhouse rolled through Paris, Milan, Berlin, and several other European cities. Prince chased his jazz jones jamming on the Charlie Parker chestnut "Now's the Time" with Matt Fink, Eric Leeds, drummer Sheila E., and the rest of the *Sign o' the Times* band regularly during the tour. That core quartet

later made up the Madhouse band of *16*, recorded in one week at Prince's home studio and the newly opened Paisley Park Studios from July 30 to August 2. The thirty-seven-minute album hit stores three months later, on November 18.

Wearing a skintight yellow polka-dotted dress, ankle-length red gloves, and red high heels with a raspberry beret, *16* cover girl Maneca Lightner leaned against a Depression-era car gripping a tommy gun. A bank features in the background. (Lightner robs a bank in the video for "Thirteen," flanked by future NPG dancers, the Game Boyz.) The album *16* failed to chart in *Billboard* at all, but the music was just as quirky and distinctive as its predeccesor.

To wit: Frank Zappa's fictional vocalist Suzy Creamcheese, aka Pamela Zarubica, is sampled on the very first track, "Nine." In-between jazz-funky snatches of "Chopsticks" and "The Sound of Music" is the voice of Creamcheese laughing out the word "bizarre," from Zappa band the Mothers of Invention's 1969 "Our Bizarre Relationship." (Check for her on "Bob George" and "Lovesexy" too—bizarre, indeed.) Francis Ford Coppola's *The Godfather* is another *16* staple. Lines from actors James Caan, Salvatore Corsitto, and Jack Woltz are sampled for "Thirteen," "Eleven," and "Sixteen," respectively. More of an instrumental funk album than a jazz record, *16* included Sheila E. and bassist Levi Seacer Jr. ("Ten," "Eleven," and "Fifteen") as well as Matt Fink ("Sixteen"), but Prince and Leeds dominated. "I thought Prince's drumming on 'Sixteen' was among his best recorded drum work," Leeds says.

"My personal opinion about Madhouse is, it's truly a fusion of jazz, R&B, and funk instrumental influences," Matt Fink concludes. "It doesn't strike me as being the kind of fusion jazz that people like Chick Corea or Herbie Hancock did. It was kind of a new fusion. Eric brings in that real jazzy, almost beboppy horn stuff, and brought in the funk. They got innovative by using sampled sounds and things from specialized sound effects. But when you really listen to the music, it's more of a funk-oriented thing to me, like funk jazz.

"Do you agree?" ●

LA COSA NOSTRA

The Family

by **Alan Leeds**

Members of Prince's mid-'80s spin-off project, the Family, have reunited under the guise of fDeluxe.

Once upon a time, Prince picked up the shambles of the post–*Purple Rain* Time and turned it into the Family. But this was no natural evolution. That this family's patriarch preferred to bury the name rather than see his offspring carry it forward is just a sidebar. fDeluxe, né the Family, is a group on the verge of a most unlikely comeback.

The story began with Prince and the Time's Morris Day parting ways. That left Jesse Johnson, the band's guitar maven, halfheartedly rehearsing the group until Prince abruptly flipped the switch. "Let's get some of that Duran Duran money," he famously told me, Johnson, and a stunned, baby-faced Time keyboardist, St. Paul Peterson. Paul would be the front man, alongside Susannah Melvoin, the attractive twin sister of Revolution guitarist Wendy. Jesse was disillusioned enough to quickly give notice. But Prince was nothing if not impulsive and stubbornly confident. Soon, he was in the studio teaching Paul and Susannah the lyrics to songs like "High Fashion," "Mutiny" (guess what inspired that one), "The Screams of Passion," and the gorgeous "Nothing Compares 2 U."

Prince knew the project needed more than Paul and Susannah. He grabbed the Time's Jellybean Johnson and Jerome Benton out of the unemployment line—they were shoo-ins for the new band. The ringer was saxophonist Eric Leeds (full disclosure required—yes, he's my adopted son and I'm proud, damnit). Leeds had mysteriously surfaced within the Revolution during *Purple Rain* tour performances after his snail-mail audition tape arrived too late for the Sheila E. gig he was chasing.

The short version is that the Family enjoyed a mid-chart hit in 1985 with "The Screams of Passion" and debuted with a volcanic gig at First Avenue in Minneapolis. Days later, their mentor was in France shooting *Under the Cherry Moon*. Just when the Family should have been aggressively promoted and marketed, they went ignored by their very own, umm, "family." Peterson took a promising deal with MCA, and the project evaporated into thin air.

The record that Questlove embraces as one of the greatest "lost" albums of all time is a cult favorite. The irony, of course, is that one Sinead O'Connor enjoyed a huge hit with "Nothing Compares 2 U." It should be a tribute when a band's song is successfully covered and revived, but what must it have felt like when your own, original version never got the time of day? Ask Susannah Melvoin. "Weird, just weird. I was like, 'Hey, at least let us have the hit first.'"

And that would be the end of this tale except for the fact that the Prince-inspired Minneapolis scene remained uniquely nepotistic. Peterson, Johnson, and Leeds seldom went more than a couple months without jamming at some local club. In 2003, Sheila E. organized a benefit concert that brought the Family together for a much-delayed second performance. Then Rabbi Questlove insisted they play at one of his hot-ticket Grammy parties, convincing the band they still had a life if they wanted it.

Paul and Susannah began writing. Then Eric and Jellybean found themselves in the studio arranging and adding parts. The Family was back. Oops, not quite. Enter Papa Prince who claimed ownership of the name and insisted that any revival could only be under his direction. But that wasn't the plan. Long out of the nest, the band was eager to fly on their own wings. It's unclear whether Prince really owns the trademark, but as long as he's convinced he does, the band decided it wasn't worth the drama (or expense) to wrestle a bunch of purple lawyers. (Jellybean, who also tours with the Time, aka Original 7even, calls himself the no-name drummer, pointing out that he's in two bands, neither of which Prince allows to use their original names.)

fDeluxe dropped their new CD to an avid critical reception in Europe and the U.K. (a full page in London's *Sunday Times!*). The U.S. has been slower to clock this band of adult musicians whose last record was nearly three decades ago, but red-hot showcase gigs in New York, L.A., Minneapolis, and Oakland were packed. The group tours Europe in early 2012. The band may not exemplify the cliché of a family "that plays together stays together." But one thing's for sure, whatever name they play under, the *music* is definitely together! ◗

Guitarist Jesse Johnson was an instrumental part of the Time, crafting some of their most well-known songs before departing on a solo career. While continuing to collaborate with idols like Sly Stone or jam with protégés like D'Angelo, Johnson charts new territory while staking a claim to the Minneapolis funk-rock sound that Prince and his affiliates created.

ROCK STAR

Jesse Johnson

by **Michael A. Gonzales**

Sipping from a glass of sparkling water, guitarist Jesse Johnson, who released his fifth solo disc, *Verbal Penetration*, in 2008, sits in the living room of Philadelphia radio personality Dyana Williams. Unlike other 1980s funk-rock-soul artists, whose hard living translates into weathered features, fifty-year-old Jesse Johnson still looks smooth.

The night before, the divorced father of four stood on-stage of the Hard Rock Café, rocking a pink paisley shirt and looking as fresh as he did in 1981 when debuting with Minneapolis funkateers the Time. Taking requests from the audience, he played his solo hits including "Baby Let's Kiss" and "Be Your Man."

"The people who listened to my music back in the '80s hold me up to a standard," Jesse explains. "I represent a cool time in their lives, so if I look good and sound good, it's like a reflection of them."

Since buying his first guitar after hearing Hendrix's "Red House" when he was thirteen, Johnson has taken his art seriously. Raised by a dad who kept a box of 78s and turned baby boy on to Lightin' Hopkins and Albert King, Jesse was already a fan of the blues. "But it wasn't until I heard 'Red House' that I knew what I wanted to do."

Living with foster parents in East St. Louis after his own folks divorced, Jesse mowed lawns until he had enough money to go to Grandpa's music store and pay thirty-nine dollars for a Norma. "It was a really cheap guitar, but to me it was the equivalent of a '57 original Stratocaster. To me, it was amazing."

For Johnson, learning the instrument was pure pleasure. "Once I figured it out, it came easy." His foster parents gifted him an amp, and he practiced in their basement. "When you first start playing an instrument, it's such a love, and that's what you don't want to lose." Through high school, he soaked up influences that included Eddie Hazel and Curtis Mayfield.

"My mother played the Impressions' 'Keep on Pushing' so much, the grooves of the 45 literally turned to dust." After graduation, Johnson returned to his hometown of Rock Island, Illinois. Living with his real dad, he played in a rock cover band at local club the Yankee Clipper.

"We played fifty weeks a year, and the band lived upstairs where there used to be a massage parlor." Jamming with visiting rockers passing through town, Jesse recalls, "I played with everybody from Journey to AC/DC, and they all asked the same question: 'What are you doing here?'" In the spring of 1981, he finally broke out.

Three hundred and sixty-one miles from home, Jesse Johnson stepped off the Trailways without a plan. "The only reason I wound up in Minneapolis was because I didn't have the fare for Los Angeles," Johnson laughs, thirty years after hopping on the bus carrying a suitcase and his white Flying V guitar.

"I didn't know a soul, so I got a room at the YMCA." Luckily, things happened quickly. "By chance, I met a woman who got me a few modelling gigs. I did print ads for music stores, holding guitars and things."

Yet, it wasn't until auditioning for Enterprise, a band featuring Morris Day on drums and Sue Ann Carwell on lead vocals, that he began making progress. While Jesse aced the audition, the band's life was short.

"Although *Dirty Mind* was out, I'd never heard of Prince, but when Morris told me that the bass player André Cymone was leaving, I said, 'Well, I play bass; you should tell him I'd like to audition.' Morris never told him that, but he did tell him I was a bad guitar player. So, Prince invited me to his show at First Avenue."

Jesse later joined the Enterprise members at their basement rehearsal space. "When Prince came downstairs, I said, 'The show was really cool. You dig Hendrix, huh?' Prince answered, 'I never watch him.' Morris stood behind him gesturing for me to shut up, but instead, I said, 'You lying motherfucker.' Prince

stared at me for a few seconds and then fell on the floor laughing." Jesse was hired on the spot as the guitarist for Prince's side project.

"At first, it was going to be me and Morris calling ourselves the Nerve, and we were going to be a Black version of Hall & Oates. But, then Prince had another idea." Pulling together players from various groups, Prince constructed a blazing band. "Jimmy Jam [keyboards] was in Mind Over Matter, while Terry Lewis [bass], Jellybean Johnson [drums], and Monte Moir [keyboards] played with Flyte Time," Johnson says. "When Prince put us all together, that's how the Time came to be."

Prince's soulful vision was rooted in the sharp-suited R&B tradition rather than the freaky electro direction his own music was taking post–*Dirty Mind*. "A few days later, Prince took Morris on the road. When Morris left, he was wearing jeans, sneakers, a regular shirt and an Afro. When he came back, he looked like the Morris we know today. He was completely different. I never saw him in jeans again."

Although Prince and Morris recorded all the songs for the Time's self-titled debut, including the singles "Get It Up" and "Cool," by midsummer, Jesse Johnson's picture was on the cover of a Warner Bros. release three months after his arrival.

For the next three years, through much drama and strife, the Time developed into a dynamic band. "The Time belonged to a new era of funk," writes Per Nilsen in *DanceMusicSexRomance*. "Their raunchy new wave funk, with its pared-down synth-dominated sound was far removed from the often horn-boosted and elaborate funk music of the latter part of the '70s."

The Time rehearsed every day, tightening their choreography and preparing for the road. "During that first tour, we didn't know what we were doing," Johnson admits. "We didn't have the right gear or clothes. We were just learning, and it showed. We looked at our performance videos, and we looked like fools."

After their sophomore release, *What Time Is It*, dropped the following year, the Time and Vanity 6 opened the *Controversy* tour. Prince hired André Cymone's sister, Sylvia, to make their clothes. Tailoring

Johnson's first pink suit, the color became his trademark. "Prince wouldn't let us use all the lights onstage. But, wearing that pink suit, the audience could always see me, so it worked out perfectly."

Accompanying Vanity 6 from behind a curtain, the Time then ran offstage and was ready "in eleven minutes" for their own set. Yet, instead of sharing the profits from the shows and merchandising, Prince paid the group a small salary. "We were angry, because we were so broke," Jesse says. "We were all pretty pissed, and that energy came out in our show. We were out for blood."

It was obvious that the cool boys were hot and Prince was becoming jealous. The next year, during the *1999* tour, budding producers Terry Lewis and Jimmy Jam snuck away to cut "Just Be Good to Me" with the S.O.S. Band. Caught in a freak snowstorm in Atlanta, the duo missed a show.

"They rejoined us, and we finished the tour," Jesse says. "Afterwards, we were at Sunset Sound preparing for our next album, and Prince told Morris he was going to fine them. Instead, he fired them. Personally, I think the Time was just too good, and he wanted to ruin and weaken it. One way of doing it was to break us up."

Jesse contributed "Jungle Love" and "The Bird" to the Time's third album, *Ice Cream Castle*; both songs were in *Purple Rain*. "I played tapes of my songs for him, and Prince would literally start laughing," Jesse says. "He'd call Morris over and be like, 'Listen to this, listen to this,' and they both laughed. When I bought him the music for 'Jungle Love,' he wasn't laughing anymore."

On the set of *Purple Rain*, the friction between the two camps was obvious. Mark Cardenas, one of the two keyboardists hired to replace Jimmy Jam, says from his home in Seattle, "There was always some bullshit between Morris and Prince. After we finished filming, Morris went to Los Angeles and didn't contact anyone. We were supposed to go on the *Purple Rain* tour, but instead Prince took Shelia E. I got a platinum record in the mail, but that was it." By the end of the year, Cardenas joined the Jesse Johnson Revue.

"Terry and Jimmy were gone," Jesse says. "Then, Morris split, and I was still there. Prince wanted to put Paul Peterson in front, and when I asked if I was going

sing or write more, he said no. I couldn't see the point of staying just to get pushed further down the totem pole. After *Purple Rain*, I was more famous, but still broke, so leaving was an easy decision."

Even when the Time was in their prime, Jesse Johnson worked on becoming a better producer. Living at Prince's purple pad on Lake Riley, he had access to the studio. "What I learned from Prince about the studio was there are absolutely no rules. Stuff people said about spending a million dollars on equipment and going to recording school, he flushed all that down the toilet.

"When I first moved in, he had garbage speakers and a sixteen-track board that was made for live sound; it wasn't even a recording board. The studio itself was just a regular bedroom, but whenever you walked in, Prince was recording some incredible stuff. He always worked in the middle of the night on some vampire shit, but dude knew how to make records."

Susan Rogers, a maintenance engineer hired in 1983 and later recruited as Prince's recording engineer, remembers Jesse helping her transition. "Prince was spending a lot of time in L.A. [at Sunset Sound] working on *Purple Rain*, so Jesse basically showed me how Prince liked to have the instruments miked and how to capture the right sounds. He was a real friend."

Signing to A&M Records in 1984, the same year he played guitar on Shalamar's single, "Dead Giveaway," Jesse built his Jungle Love studio in the basement of his new townhouse. "Prince sold me his Soundcraft recording board for $23,000," he remembers. "He used that same board to record *1999*, *What Time Is It*, and *Purple Rain*. I went to the Civic Center where he was doing a dress rehearsal for the *Purple Rain* tour and gave him a check. That's how I was able to finish the studio."

Jesse recorded his trio of '80s albums—*Jesse Johnson Revue* (1985), *Shockadelica* (1986), and *Every Shade of Love* (1988)—at Jungle Love. While the debut featured "Be Your Man" and "I Want My Girl," Johnson admits, "There was no real thought process to making those early tracks, because it was something I hadn't done before. I was doing stuff, listening to it, and hoping it sounded presentable."

It didn't help that his girlfriend wasn't a fan. "She told me that I ruined songs," he laughs. "I'd have a great bass line and drumbeat on the rough. Then I'd add some keyboards, not knowing what I was doing. My girlfriend would hear it and say, 'You messed it up.' She was right; I had to bring up my keyboard game."

Engineer Susan Rogers, who now teaches at Berklee in Boston, says, "In the beginning, Jesse wasn't a natural front man or lyricist, but I think he is being modest about his abilities in the studio. Other than being a strong musician, he is also a talented arranger and producer."

Working to establish solo success, Jesse agreed to open for New Edition in 1985. "It was like when Hendrix opened for the Monkees," he laughs. "The audience was mostly little kids. It was very uncomfortable, but we had to stay on the road until the record climbed the charts."

A year later, Jesse worked with funk-rock pioneer Sly Stone on *Shockadelica*'s first single, "Crazay." Says Jesse, "Sly impressed me with his grasp of technology; he was messing with sequencers that I couldn't even turn on. After the video shoot, he played me some new music. My mind couldn't handle how incredible it was. Whatever you think is funky, Sly was funkier." Prince later sampled Sly's "Crazay" voice on the 12-inch of "Housequake (7 Minutes Moquake)."

Not understanding why Jesse didn't create a title track, Prince recorded his own "Shockadelica" song. "My album was already out, but Prince tried to convince me to record his track for the next pressing. I didn't think that was fair to people who had already bought the album, so I didn't put it out. Prince told me, 'Well, I'll put it out, and when people think of 'Shockadelica,' they'll think of me.'" The song was on the B-side of "If I Was Your Girlfriend."

While there were rumors that Sly had gotten Johnson hooked on drugs, he dismisses the myth. "Sly never even did any of that stuff around me. I've never been curious about drugs; I've never even smoked a cigarette." Citing 1973's *Fresh* as his favorite Sly album, Jesse continues, "We later worked on a bunch of stuff together, but nothing ever came of it."

Johnson did outside production for various artists including Janet Jackson and Ta Mara and the Seen, while also contributing to the soundtracks of Brat Pack classics *The Breakfast Club* ("Heart Too Hot to Hold," 1985) and *Pretty in Pink* ("Get to Know Ya," 1986). "Director John Hughes was from Illinois and a fan of the Time," Jesse says. "He requested me himself."

In 1988, Johnson released his third and last A&M album, *Every Shade of Love*. "I did a fourth record, but [it] was shelved. This was when new jack swing was big, and they wanted me to make records that sounded like that; they wanted me to work with new-jack producers, but I wasn't interested."

Instead, Jesse delivered *In the Real Life Mode*, an album that was never released. "It was a scary, angry record. It was a depressing time, and the music on there reflected that darkness," Jesse says. "One song was called 'Perpetrator.' I'm actually glad it didn't come out."

Waiting for the A&M contract to expire, eight years passed before he released the electric rawness of *Bare My Naked Soul* in 1996. "One of the best (black) rock albums of all times," writer Kandia Crazy Horse proclaimed in the book *Rip It Up: The Black Experience in Rock 'n' Roll*.

Thirty years after leaving Rock Island to become a rock star, Jesse Johnson is still striving. Recently, he has been jamming with his new friend D'Angelo. "We've played together on a bunch of stuff," Johnson says. "He'll play bass or drums or I'll play bass. We just jam and record to get licks and things."

In addition, Jesse recently worked with the original Time members on their first disc since *Pandemonium* (1990)—the Original 7ven's *Condensate* was released in October 2011. Recording at his home in Los Angeles and at the Flyte Time studio in Santa Monica, he says, "To this day, we're all pretty tight. Always laughing and having fun. Our thing always was, we'd do other things, but in the end, we would always come back to the Time." ⊙

Michael A. Gonzales's essays have been cited in *Da Capo Best Music Writing 2008, 2009*, and *2010*. He wishes to thank Dyana Williams for using her influence to make this interview happen.

BIG TIME

Morris Day

by **Dean Van Nguyen**

Morris Day is an icon of the Minneapolis-drenched sound of '80s R&B. Beginning his career as a talented drummer but winding up as the front man for the Time, Day was an important piece in the Prince puzzle and worked hard to create a bigger-than-life persona that still resonates to this day. Eventually rising from the shadow of the Purple One, Day was able to establish himself as a shining star in his own right.

In the late 1970s, Minneapolis experienced a flow of new musical talent that ensured their unique mesh of R&B, funk, and rock would be at the forefront of American pop music for the next decade. Even more incredible was that this burst of creativity, tantamount to an explosion, was almost entirely localized to just a handful of cliques. The scene became fully formed as childhood friends built their rep almost simultaneously. Bandleaders adopted a "never leave a good man behind" mentality as they brought their friends up with them, occasionally swapped band members, and cut a huge body of great music.

A key figure among this surge of new talent that emerged from one half of the Twin Cities, Morris Day was enigmatic, likable, infinitely talented, and blessed with a knack of being in the right place at the right time. As a teenager, he established himself as an important figure in Prince's fledgling music career, almost accidentally becoming the front man of the Purple One's side project group, the Time. With the band, Morris established himself as a star in his own right. Appearing in the Prince-produced vanity project that was the movie *Purple Rain*, his humorous performance as a cranked-up, fictionalized version of himself stole the show from Prince's moody character, "The Kid," and his backing band the Revolution.

With this star turn, a reputation of upstaging their mentor when opening his gigs, and hit singles like "Jungle Love," the Time were on top of the world. But in 1985, at the peak of their popularity, and amidst a series of bust-ups and fall-outs, Morris put the final nail in the band's coffin. Seeking the artistic credibility he felt he was owed, he dissolved his group to pursue a solo career outside of Prince's shadow.

"I could play ten times better than Bobby Z, but we ain't gonna get into that," asserts Morris. Clearly, he's still smarting from Prince's decision to recruit another drummer for the Revolution. In fact, throughout our phone interview, he's hesitant to give anyone else any credit for his achievements. But I sense it's not an egotistical streak that's in him, just a symptom of a career where his many talents have been underappreciated. While he gave the impression onstage as being a showman first and musician second, Morris was a talented instrumentalist in his own right, having been enamored by music from a very young age.

"I remember we had our first color TV set back in '64, and I would watch *Bandstand*, and acts like the Four Tops and James Brown would come on," remembers Morris. "I just gravitated towards music, which I figured I was put here to do that, because, really, nobody in my family was into music necessarily."

To save her wooden kitchen utensils that Morris would often break from his incessant drumming on the furniture, his mother bought him a drum set. Within a year, he was playing in his first bands, but it wasn't until he hooked up with a school-mate that things really began to take off. "I first got involved with Prince in high school," says Morris. "I saw his band Grand Central play one day in the lunch room after school. These guys were fourteen, fifteen years old, and I'd never heard anything like it for guys that age. Prince was playing, like, Santana solos! I was really mesmerized."

Morris struck up a friendship with Grand Central's bass player, André Cymone, who himself would go on to have a string of hits in the early '80s. "He didn't know that I played drums," laughs Morris. "We skipped school a time or two and went to my mom's. I had my drums set up with a big speaker behind them. I got on the drums and played, and when I finished, André's looking at me with eyes all big like, 'Man, I didn't know you played like that.'"

Morris was soon instilled as Grand Central's new drummer, but before the group could achieve any major success in their own right, Prince broke from the band and signed a contract with Warner Bros. Records as a solo artist. Morris had hoped to be enlisted into his newly formed backing band, the Revolution, but discovered the spot had already been filled. However, when Prince asked to record an original composition of Day's titled "Partyup"—subsequently credited to Prince—for the groundbreaking 1980 album *Dirty Mind*, the door was opened for Morris to help form a new act. "He was like, 'I can either give you some money, or I'll help you put a band together.' So I said, 'I'll take the band.'

That's really how the Time was born."

A clause in Prince's contract with Warner Bros. allowed him to recruit and produce other artists for the label. With his own music quickly evolving away from the traditional Minneapolis sound, he wanted to establish a group that could serve as an outlet for the genre he had helped create. Writing and producing for the Time under different pseudonyms would allow him to continue to make the music he loved—away from the pop world's watchful eye. He quickly enlisted Minneapolis group Flyte Time to form the bulk of the band. Their lineup included Monte Moir, Jimmy Jam, Terry Lewis, and Jellybean Johnson. Alexander O'Neal had been the band's singer, but soon departed over contractual disagreements with Prince. In need of a front man and with no other options, Morris was reluctantly talked into coming from behind the drum kit to take front-and-center stage behind the mic.

Having never fronted a band before, Morris needed to learn quickly. Without the experience of being a polished live singer, he began to construct his own unique onstage persona, and, naturally, his charisma shined through. "I'd come up to sing a couple of slow songs, but Prince said, 'Be cool; put your hand in your pocket.' So I tried that and just kept working at it and kept coming up with different things. We starting coming up with songs like 'Cool,' and it just evolved into a whole way of me doing business. It started from, 'Okay, I'll put my hand in my pocket, and I'll walk a lot.' And [it] went from there."

Guitarist Jesse Johnson, a longtime collaborator of Morris's, was added, but the Time's lineup had not yet been complete. As Morris explains, the band, and the final element of his persona, came together off the cuff. "Jerome [Benton] was always around, because he's Terry Lewis's brother. We were at rehearsal one time, and in the song 'Cool,' I say, 'Somebody bring me a mirror.' Jerome runs into the bathroom and snatches the mirror off the wall and ran up to me, and that was it. From that day on, he was in the band." Indeed, vanity was humorously incorporated into the Morris Day image. The idea of looking, acting, and simply being cool was embedded into his persona. His permed hair never had a lock

The Time from their 1981 self-titled release. (clockwise from bottom left) Terry Lewis, Jimmy Jam, Jellybean Johnson, Monte Moir, Jesse Johnson, and Morris Day. Photo by Allen Beaulieu.

out of the place, and the whole band always dressed formally onstage, drawing inspiration from the zoot suits of their grandfather's generation.

The band released three albums in quick succession: *The Time*, *What Time Is It?*, and *Ice Cream Castles*. With Prince calling the shots, the rest of the band's input in the studio was limited, though the misconception that Prince did everything bar sing lead vocals has long irked the band. In a 1996 web-chat interview, when asked if Prince, Morris, and Revolution guitarist/vocalist Dez Dickerson were the only contributors to their debut record, Jerome simply snapped: "No, it's not true. Next question." About his own involvement in the Time's early discography, Morris is quick to set the record straight. "I had a lot of creative input. I played the drums and helped craft a lot of the stuff. I was there every moment of putting the song together. Not to take credit for Prince; it was his vision early on. It was an alter-ego thing, things he felt he couldn't get away with the direction he was going in."

That direction was towards superstardom, which would finally be confirmed upon the release of his megafilm and soundtrack project in 1984, *Purple Rain*.

Morris remembers: "One day, Prince was like, 'We're making a movie.' I was like, 'Okay, fine.' So I started going to acting class and dancing class and all sorts of silly stuff. I got kicked out of acting class, because I kept clowning around and the guys said I was disrupting it for everybody. That's pretty much [how I] did the best in the movie, by cutting up."

Morris's portrayal as a brash, womanizing nightclub owner brought the Time to a wider audience, but again he felt his contribution to the project was underappreciated. "I got paid fifty grand for being in *Purple Rain*. I wrote all my own lines, so again, my creative input was overlooked, but you know, it was a great experience. It was an innocent effort, because we had no idea that it was going to go where it went, or take our careers."

Purple Rain would prove to be the peak of the Time's popularity, but by the time it was released, the band had already fractured. A rift between Prince and the band began

to develop, with rumors that some members had grown weary of their lack of input into the music and being underpaid. Things came to a head in 1983 during the *1999* tour when Terry Lewis and Jimmy Jam, who had already started what would prove to be a hugely successful career as producers, were stranded in Atlanta by a blizzard and failed to make it to a show in San Antonio. Prince was forced into playing bass for Lewis offstage, while Jerome mimed the actions in front of the crowd. The duo was subsequently fired for this indiscretion. It was a huge blow for Morris.

"At the time when Terry and Jimmy were kicked out of the band, we were still signed to Prince's production company, so he basically fired them. I was very unhappy about that. So then we brought in new members. Back in the day when I was a young guy, that was one of my pet peeves about music; I didn't like bands switching members. Once I started to like the band, it wasn't the same to me when they switched members, and when we started doing that, I just never felt the same way about the band. I didn't feel the camaraderie; I didn't feel I knew these guys when we performed. Jesse Johnson had struck a deal quietly; I found out that he had done an album and signed to A&M. So all my key guys are just not going to be around me anymore. So I opted out. I went and struck a solo deal myself and said, 'So be it.'"

Morris Day had cut his teeth in the Time, but Prince's tight grip on the band restricted his input of the final product. As a solo artist, he was keen to stretch his creative muscles, even turning down the Purple One's offer to nurture his fledgling career. "When I was still signed to [Prince's] production company, I asked if I could do a solo record, and he said, 'Yeah, but I have to be the executive producer.' Well, with Prince, I knew what that meant; I wasn't going to get any input, so I was like, 'That ain't gonna work.' I was writing songs all day, all night. It was the peak of my creativity, and a lot of stuff I submitted that I wanted to go on a [Time] record, for whatever reason, it wouldn't make it on. So I needed to get this out of my system."

Rather than working with Prince, he signed a deal that allowed his album to come out on Warner Bros., but with creative control solely at his door. As well as singing, he would produce, compose, and arrange the entire record. Released in 1985, *The Color of Success* marked a huge increase in responsibility for Morris.

At first glance, *The Color of Success* doesn't appear to be a great change of pace for Morris. The cover, where he looks typically sharp dressed standing in front of a city backdrop, reveals he wasn't interested in a total image change. Also, with a six-song structure, it employs the same format used by the Time. "I didn't feel like I necessarily needed to separate myself from where I came from, but I just thought that naturally that would happen, because I did things differently," says Morris.

These differences are apparent to the trained ear. The production is mostly built around soft synth loops, far more minimalist than the Time's often expansive arrangements. Slightly less of a party record than his band's output, it's a toy chest of different ideas and genres, hoarded away from a lifetime of music and a career in a band where his artistic input was often overlooked.

Thematically, *The Color of Success* is about striking out on one's own. Opening with the title track and a small portion of "Over the Rainbow" from *The Wizard of Oz,* it mirrors a similar trick that opened *Ice Cream Castles,* ensuring the past is acknowledged. "I just kinda liked that vibe," says Morris. "Coming in real soft and angelic, and hittin' 'em with a hard groove right after that."

But it is in this title track that the record's mentality is summed up, with the lyric "Dark wind is gone / Sun is shining." Referencing the cloudy days of the Time's demise, Morris was very much drawing a line in the sand. The weather motif also represents him psychologically exorcising himself from his *Purple Rain* days. "It was a play on that whole thing," he says. "I had to get it out."

In the studio, Day was adjusting to his newfound responsibility with some aplomb. "It was kind of a trip, because 'Oak Tree,' for instance, it was eight minutes long. So we did the track, I had the guys come in, musicians that I used. Then they left, and I'm sitting there in the studio, I was like,

'Now I gotta layer all this, and I gotta make it make sense.' [*laughs*] I wrote the hook and got past the verses. I felt the responsibility at that point, but once I got past that, I started having fun with it."

The album also features a good dollop of guitar from some famous friends. "I insisted on having good guitar work on the record. It was good musicianship, period. I used [session] guitar player [Tony Berg], and Roland Bautista from Earth, Wind & Fire, I used on "Don't Wait for Me." And some of it was suggestions from them. These guys came in, and I didn't know if they knew how I wanted things played, and they killed it."

While the *Color of Success* was something of a learning curve, Morris was keen to take the lessons he had learned and expand them even further on follow-up record *Daydreaming* in 1987. To help with the process, he recruited Terry Lewis and Jimmy Jam to coproduce two tracks, "Fishnet" and "Love Is a Game." "It was suggested that maybe I go to them for a couple of songs," Day says of the two, who were hot property after producing Janet Jackson's *Control* the year before. "In my mind, [their] production [quality] was up, but I think I was more in a bigger production state of mind when I got to that record." It was this scaled-up mentality that spawned "Fishnet," his most radio-friendly solo track to date. Its pounding drumbeat, infectious keyboard riff, and sexed-up lyrics sent it to number one on the soul singles chart for two weeks.

Also noteworthy is "A Man's Pride," almost operatic in its approach. Morris used a twenty-six-piece orchestra to bring his vision to fruition. "My ex-wife wrote the lyrics with me," he says, "but I wrote the music. It was just something that was rolling around in my head for some reason. I always think that songs come from God or the universe; that was what just came to me at that time. I had done a song on the piano at home on a four-track, and I put the strings on it, and I was like, 'Wow, this is really nice.' It could be a lot bigger than just doing things the way I usually do, which is using basic keyboards, guitar, bass. I wanted to make this something unique and really big."

Despite being a record with seemingly

more commercial appeal, *Daydreaming* only managed a number forty-one spot on the *Billboard* charts, four places below the peak position of *Color of Success*. When asked if he considers this phase of his career to be a success, Morris is pragmatic. "Personally, it was. I don't think I produced the numbers I wanted to sell, but I think I made the creative statement that I wanted to make."

As well as producers Terry Lewis and Jimmy Jam, the Time were also credited on "Fishnet" and "Love Is a Game," and the original lineup would be reunited soon after. But was it working on *Daydreaming* that sparked the full-blown reunion? "Yeah, I think that might have been what spurred it. We had started a project with Prince, Jerome, and myself, and it was going to be called *Corporate World*. Around the time we finished *Graffiti Bridge*, we did the whole record, and then Terry and Jimmy sort of came out of the woodwork and wanted to be involved, and I think that's how we ended up with a full-scale reunion."

Were you happy to continue your career in the Time?

"It was sort of double edged," Day remembers. "Because—unlike the early days where we were getting screwed anyway, but it wasn't as political—that [reunion] became a political nightmare, because everybody had their attorneys, their pieces of pie they were fighting for. It wasn't the same."

The band spent much of the '90s again chopping and changing members, and Morris attempted to update his image by cutting off his trademark permed hair and releasing *Guaranteed*, a hip-hop album in 1992 that was poorly received. However, there would be a resurgence in 2001, when director Kevin Smith cast the group in his movie *Jay and Silent Bob Strike Back*. In the film, Jay proclaims that he "and Silent Bob modeled our whole fucking lives around Morris Day and Jerome." The movie ends with a rousing rendition of "Jungle Love."

"At the time, my sons were teenagers, and I'd pick them up from school," says Morris. "I was pretty much known to their friends as their dad. 'Hey, that's Kevin and Darren's dad.' After *Jay and Silent Bob* hit the streets, they were like, 'Hey, that's Morris Day.' " ◗

WITNESS TO THE FUNK
Larry Graham

by **Allen Thayer**

From Sly and the Family Stone to his own band Graham Central Station, master funk bassist and singer Larry Graham single-handedly revolutionized the instrument while influencing many musical genres and countless musicians. A chance invitation to jam with disciple Prince has led to the formation of a deep spiritual bond that goes beyond music and into their relentless pursuit of the Truth.

When I was coming up, you couldn't get a gig if you couldn't thump and pluck like Graham. But it wasn't just his technique; the spirit that he approaches music with is incredible. The way he thumps octaves is sick. Everything has attitude and inflections, like a blues guitarist on bass.[1]

–Marcus Miller

Probably when Jesus went to the people, some of the people recognized him, but a lot of the time, people didn't. With us, it's the same thing. Prince never tried to go out wearing a disguise, 'cause if somebody recognizes him, then all the more so they wanna know what's up, what got him into this?

–Larry Graham, on evangelizing door-to-
door with his "spiritual brother," Prince

If Prince is Jesus in the hypothetical funk pantheon, then Larry Graham is Saint Paul. Jesus might have been the idea man, but Paul was the guy that wrote a good chunk of the New Testament and made it his life's mission to spread Jesus's teachings far and wide. Like the Christian hierarchy, the celestial-funk org chart has some quirks to it, whereby Larry's old bandmate, Sly Stone (né Stewart), also appears as the star-child funk messiah, obviously in an earlier incarnation than Prince (hey, it's no less confusing than trying to make sense of the Holy Ghost). Naturally, the "Godfather" James Brown is God, the Father of Funk.

Like Paul, Larry's got a knack for keeping company with larger-than-life figures like Sly and Prince. These associations help amplify his personal message of love, friendship, faith, and funk, but it also obscures his own formidable works: inventing and popularizing the funk bass style; anchoring iconic funk and soul singles as a founding member, bass player, and vocalist in Sly and the Family Stone; leading the first R&B band, Graham Central Station, signed to Warner Bros. and the first also to earn a gold record; and his indisputable influence on the past and present canon of funk music.

A Family Affair

Larry Graham Jr. was born in Beaumont, Texas, but his family settled in Oakland, California, by the time he was two years old. While he was primarily raised by his grandmother, his parents' preoccupation with music clearly seeped into young Larry's consciousness. Larry's father gave him his first guitar at age eleven, and the young Graham taught himself how to play the thing, claiming that he "had it down" by age fifteen. Around this time, Larry's mother, Dell Graham, moved back to the Bay Area after an extended residency in Hawaii. Dell formed the Dell Graham Trio with Larry on guitar and one of his friends on drums.

The trio played clubs and lounges throughout the Bay Area doing a mix of classics and current pop hits, five to six nights a week. With a tip jar on top of the piano, the trio satisfied any request that came their way. "It was really good, because you had to learn all the standards," Larry remembers. This regular gig with his mom gave Larry the opportunity to hone his vocal talents. "I had to cover all the male stuff like Tony Bennett, Frank Sinatra, Billy Eckstine, Nat King Cole, and she would cover the Dinah Washington, Sarah Vaughan [songs], and we had all the bases covered."

During a residency at the Escort Club in Redwood City, Larry discovered the house organ and began using the bass pedals with his feet while playing the guitar and singing. Before long, the organ crapped out, leaving the trio sounding hollow. "Once you have bottom," Larry says in his deep baritone, "you can't go back." The trio trudged through a few more gigs while waiting for the organ to get fixed. When Larry found out it was irreparable,

he rented a bass guitar in order to get that bottom back.

Note that Larry rented the bass. This was a temporary fix, so he never bothered to learn the proper technique, thinking they'd find a replacement organ sooner or later. "I was never interested in playing the over-hand, so-called 'correct style.' I played guitar with my fingers anyway—I rarely used a pick," Larry recalls, "So when she decided one day to get rid of the drummer, then I missed having that backbeat, so I thumped the strings to make up for not having the bass drum and plucked the strings to make up for not having the snare drum. It just sounded right. Now, if I had been listening to bass players," Larry says, "I probably would have played like everybody else."

A Whole New Thing

Larry remembers that around 1966, Sly was "probably the most popular disc jockey in the Bay Area. Everybody loved him." One of Sly's faithful listeners repeatedly insisted he check out this bass player after the DJ announced his plans to put together his own band. "[Sly] came down one night with some of his associates and heard what I was doing and invited me to join his band," Larry recounts. Sly had the good sense to ask Dell's permission first. "I talked to Moms about it," Larry says, "and she said, 'Well, I've been all over the world and did my thing [in the music business]. Why don't you check it out.'"

It takes a visionary bandleader to recruit an unknown mama's boy bass player with a bizarre technique, but in Larry, Sly recognized a kindred spirit. Here was a talented, young musician who could not only play multiple instruments and sing in multiple octaves, but judging from his intuitive and innovative approach to funking up a backbeat, Larry clearly wasn't afraid to follow his ears into uncharted territory.

Sly made it clear from the beginning that he would be the sole bandleader, but he wasn't a taskmaster in the style of James Brown, enforcing dress codes, tardi-

ness fines, or a strict adherence to a rigid musical format. "[Sly] didn't make me try to sound like bass players out there," Larry says. "He got me in the band because of what he heard at the club." And the same could be said for every other member of the band. "I think part of his genius was to allow the band to be themselves, not trying to change us up to sound like [what was playing on] the radio."

With the green light from the Family Stone to continue to do his own thang, Larry explored new sounds on the bass, drawing on his experience as a guitar player. "I thought like a guitar player, so I would plug in pedals that guitar players would normally use, and I'd experiment with them," Larry says. "I didn't have any brain blockage against doing stuff, because I was already playing what some would consider a weird way of playing the bass. I was already off the deep end. To put a fuzz on my bass, I didn't even think twice, and it sounded cool."

Luv 'n' Haight

Sly and the Family Stone released four albums between 1967 and '69, with each one moving closer to Sly's original vision of merging the rock and soul camps, uniting the "hippies" and "squares." There might not have been many squares in attendance at Woodstock, but through the subsequent film and soundtrack, the band became a phenomenon. "[Woodstock] took our concerts up a whole 'nother giant notch, to where the concerts became an experience, for the audience and for us. We started playing in this new zone we had never played in before, and it was some of the heaviest stuff I had ever been involved in."[2]

Larry compares the experience to basketball god Michael Jordan when he first dunked from the free-throw line. "Once you do that, now you know you can, and now you gotta do that again the next time. Anything less than that, it was not a good show." Following that show, the pressure to take the audience higher night after night translated into the band members, and particularly Sly, getting higher and higher

on a combination on weed, cocaine, and, ultimately, PCP.

When the band finally paused in the wake of Woodstock, and before recording 1971's *There's a Riot Goin' On*, things started to unravel as if their frenetic pace was the only thing keeping them together. Drummer Greg Errico was the first to quit. The band canceled more than a quarter (twenty-six out of eighty) of their concerts in 1970, primarily due to their leader's absence, inability, or unwillingness to perform. "There was a gig in Oakland where he didn't show up," Larry recalled to writer Joel Selvin. "I mean, I was affected by stuff like that. This is home, so if there's a no-show, I got family and friends and stuff I've got to deal with."[3] Making matters worse, Sly moved to Los Angeles, taking up residence in a Beverly Hills mansion previously occupied by Papa John Phillips. Sly decided to record the next album, *There's a Riot Goin' On*, in a mobile home parked in front of his mansion. The rest of the band still lived in the Bay Area, so popping into the studio wasn't so simple, and when they got there, they were often told to wait around for days until their contributions were requested. Larry overdubbed his bass parts on countless tracks but never played with any other Family Stones for the album.

There was no second-in-command, but if there was a rival to Sly's authority in the group it came from Larry. "Another sort of competition had Larry Graham attempting to out-macho Sly," Sly biographer Jeff Kaliss writes. "Larry's questioning of Sly's authority had surfaced during the first few hours of the band's existence, and it's arguable that his handsome, cocky stage presence, resonant vocals, and peerless bass technique later drew some of the spotlight away from Sly."[4]

"Larry was afraid," J. B. Brown, one of Sly's thugs, recalled. "The whole situation was turning on him... I think it was just the ego clash, too. I remember when I rode with him from Roanoke, Virginia, to South Carolina. It was one of them long, long rides with six limousines from one state to the next state. There we are, three to a limo cruising up the highway. I could tell it was coming at that time, because Larry was in the car going, 'This is not getting too cool.' It was an unfriendly situation. Sly would say, 'That Larry Graham.' I think Sly killed off the band. I think he figured that he could do it all anyway. He did, up to a point."[5]

"We heard that Larry Graham had got a hit man to do Sly," another of Sly's thugs, Edward "Eddie Chin" Elliot, remembered.[6] Following a disastrous show in Los Angeles where Sly couldn't figure out how to turn on his keyboard, he focused his frustration and paranoia on Larry, giving Elliot and Bubba Banks the green light to handle the situation. Back at the Cavalier Hotel after the show: "Somebody tells me that Larry and his henchmen are in the lobby," Banks recalled. "I don't know why, but I had a walking cane in my hand. I'm in the lobby, and Larry's man is there. I took the walking cane and broke it over his head... We whipped him so bad, Larry was able to escape. He got out of there quick. That's why I say I fired him. That was the end of Larry Graham."[7] Saxophonist Pat Rizzo picks up the story: "I was the one that got him and his girlfriend out of the hotel. That was fucking scary. I saved Larry's life. We got out of there just in the fucking nick of time. They were going to kill Larry. I don't know why."[8]

Larry is downright subdued when discussing what happened that night with Joel Selvin, but it's clear he regrets the way things went down. "There comes a time when somebody leaves a family situation because it is time to go... I didn't see a scene at the hotel. I heard about some negative things that went down... By that time, the changes [in the band] that had taken place were already firmly established... I was very comfortable, very satisfied with the way things were before, naturally hoping things would stay like that. But they didn't. It was time to go."[9]

'Tis Larry's Kind of Music

Sly and the remaining Family Stones released one more classic album with *Fresh*, but the musical magic was disappearing as fast as a mound of cocaine in Sly's Beverly Hills mansion. Reeling from the undignified exit from the band that he helped build, Larry retreated to his home base in Oakland. Initially, he had no intentions of returning to the stage or recording studio as a performer, still smarting from the chaos and drama that he'd witnessed on the road.

"When I left Sly and the Family Stone, I was never intending to start my own band," Larry explains. Larry's first musical project after leaving the Family Stone was a group called Hot Chocolate (not to be confused with the U.K. soul band of the same name, or the lesser-known Cleveland funk group helmed by Lou Ragland). "I put the band together built around Patryce 'Chocolate' Banks, where she's the out-front person, and I was strictly going to be the producer/writer." Larry handpicked the rest of the band from the cream of the Bay Area talent, adding Hershall "Happiness" Kennedy on keyboards, Robert "Butch" Sam on organ, Willie "Wild" Sparks on drums, and David "Dynamite" Vega on guitar.

At one of the band's early gigs at the legendary North Beach, San Francisco, club Bimbo's, Larry joined the group on-stage for the first time. "I'm there and the crowd's loving it," Larry recalls. "And folks were egging me on to sit in towards the end of the show. And when I sat in with them, it was instantly like, 'Something just happened here.' And it became obvious that their bass player was gonna lose his gig that night."

Listening to Graham Central Station's debut album from 1974, it's impossible to ignore the effortless Family Stone vibe. Larry naturally embraces the Family Stone sound, and arguably he has as much claim to that aesthetic as anyone else, excepting Sly. "Naturally, for me, [Sly and the Family Stone] would be the foundation, the standard for me," Larry explains. "So Graham Central Station was kind of like an extension of the Sly and the Family Stone tradition." Larry's group took the funk-rock hybrid and kicked it into overdrive on songs like "Tell It Like It Is," "Hair," "Release Yourself," and "The Jam."

Larry's brand of funk was loud, hard, rhythmic as all hell, but with its strong gospel and doo-wop influences and layered with Larry's positive and often spiritual lyrics, his music was heavy, yet positive, rockin' and undeniably funky, spiritual without being religious. Even before Larry's baptism in the Jehovah's Witness Christian faith in 1975, his songs explored spiritual themes, like on the mellow-funk meditation " 'Tis Your Kind of Music," from Graham Central Station's second album, 1974's *Release Yourself*.

Graham Central Station marched on until the close of the decade with a similar formula and a fluid band roster. The last couple albums of the '70s saw the Central Station billing succumb to Larry Graham as a solo artist, which was probably more accurate musically, as Larry had always recorded most of the music himself since the first GCS albums. Larry continued to pump out up-tempo funk bombs, but with his first solo release, 1980's *One in a Million You*, he unveiled a skill last showcased when gigging with his mom's group. Reaching number one on the R&B charts and number nine on the Hot 100, the title track, written by the unsung Southern soul scribe Sam Dees, allowed Larry to show off his impressive vocal range and sentimental side.

From Tie-Dyed to Paisley

For seven years during the late '80s and into the '90s, Larry and his wife, Tina, were based out of Montego Bay, Jamaica, teaching the Bible as Jehovah's Witnesses when they weren't funking it up on tour with a newly reformed Graham Central Station. With his star continuing its re-ascent, Larry found himself on a package funk and comedy tour headlined by Sinbad with a date in Tennessee. "We played Nashville, and Prince was playing at [another] venue in town, and he invited me to come to the after-show and jam," Larry told journalist Jon Bream. "And I did, which would be the first time I actually played with him."[10]

"Larry's wife came up to him and pulled an effects box and cord out of her purse," Prince remembered warmly. "Now that's love."[11] "We played and then it was like an instant connection," Larry recalls. "It was like I'd been knowing him all my life,

musically, but it was because he'd been listening to my stuff, and everywhere I went, he was right there." Listening to Prince's catalog, Sly and the Family Stone is an obvious influence on his sound and aesthetic, but Larry soon discovered "that Prince was raised up on…mostly Graham Central Station, because by then, he was playing and had his own band and stuff. In fact, he had a band called Grand Central."

After the Sinbad tour, Prince invited Larry's Graham Central Station to finish off his tour as the opening act. Prince was clearly excited to have one of his musical idols on tour with him, but more than that, the two forged a tight personal bond around a series of intense spiritual discussions. "He would ask me these questions [about the Bible] every night, and even before the show he'd be hiding around the parking lot. The more he would learn, the more he wanted to know," Larry says. Then at the culmination of the tour, Prince asked Larry's wife, Tina: "Do you like snow?"

Larry and Tina now (and for the past fourteen years) live in a little purple community called Paisley Park, twenty-five miles outside of Minneapolis. Prince lives next door. "It's cool in spring, summer, and fall," Larry says with a chuckle. In the decade and a half since Larry and Prince adopted each other, Larry's been a featured member of Prince's New Power Generation as well as opening act. Then he recorded a new album as Graham Central Station on Prince's NPG imprint. All the while, the most important role Larry plays in the purple orbit is as a spiritual mentor and friend. "Musically, there's a natural connection," Larry told Jon Bream. "Spiritually, we have a very, very close relationship. We're like spiritual brothers. He's close with all of my family. My grandkids call him Uncle Prince."[12]

Prince produced Larry's 1998 album *GCS 2000*, and Larry explains that Prince's influence is less prominent on his next album. After more than a decade of friendship and playing music together, their bond seems tighter than ever. They regularly jam together, and when they tour together, it's not uncommon to see the one jamming onstage during the other's set. Karl Coryat interviewed Prince for *Bass Player* maga-

zine in 1999, writing, "It seemed no matter what I asked, the conversation turned to either God, Larry Graham, or both—the Artist freely admitting he modeled his bass style after Graham's."[13]

"Here's a guy who has a brother hug for you every day," said Prince. "And once Larry taught me The Truth, everything changed. My agoraphobia went away. I used to have nightmares about going to the mall, with everyone looking at me strange. No more." Larry told me that these days, Prince doesn't identify with any one specific church (his religious affiliations are about as hard to keep track of as what we're supposed to call him), but when asked if it's true that he and Prince go door-to-door evangelizing, he said, "We did last Sunday."

A lasting movement of any kind, be it religious, political, or musical, usually begins with a visionary leader. But a movement rarely survives the passing of its leader without dedicated followers who can interpret and spread the movement's message. "As an artist, to know that I had an influence on Prince and other artists," Larry told Reflections in Rhythm blog, "aw, man, it does the heart good."[14] Just like the Motown's near-anonymous Funk Brothers or the rotating cast of James Brown's band, Larry Graham was instrumental in stretching soul music beyond its comfort zone, transforming the sound of popular music in the process. Future funk apostles—like Marcus Miller, Rick James, and Prince—would use Larry Graham's sound and spirit as a jumping off point to take the funk to the masses. ●

Notes
1. Rick Suchow, "Larry Graham: The Godfather of Funk Bass," *Bass Musician*, November 2010.
2. Joel Selvin, *For the Record: Sly & the Family Stone – An Oral History*, Avon Books, 1998, p. 78.
3. Ibid, p. 103.
4. Jeff Kaliss, *I Want to Take You Higher*, Backbeat Books, 2008, pp. 111–112.
5. Selvin, p. 146.
6. Ibid, p. 151.
7. Ibid.
8. Ibid, pp. 151–152.
9. Ibid, p. 152.
10. Jon Bream, "Larry Graham: Hot Fun in the Summertime," *Star Tribune*, June 17, 2010.
11. Karl Coryat, "His Highness Gets Down!," *Bass Player* magazine, November, 1999.
12. Bream.
13. Coryat.
14. Interview on reflectionsinrhythm.wordpress.com, 8/8/2010.

BEHIND THE PURPLE ROPES
Prince and the Revolution

by **Alan** and **Gwen Leeds**

Having gained heavyweight status as James Brown's
tour manager, Alan Leeds was brought on midway
through Prince's *1999* tour as a freelance replacement.
But after finding his niche within the sometimes peculiar
Prince entourage, Alan and his now wife Gwen moved to
Minneapolis to work for the artist full time. Little did they
know, they were about to witness some of the greatest
years in the history of popular music as Prince and the
Revolution busted out with the groundbreaking album and
film *Purple Rain*.

In early 1983, Prince hired tour manager Alan Leeds sight unseen. Leeds was told his selling point was having worked for James Brown. Hurried to fill the mid-tour vacancy, Prince told manager Steve Fargnoli, "Just get that James Brown guy."

A freelancer, Leeds viewed the remaining weeks of Prince's *1999* tour as just another credential on his résumé. He was looking forward to winding up many months on the road and returning home to girlfriend Gwen Gwyn in New York where she was public relations manager for the prestigious but assuredly non-rock-and-roll Hayden Planetarium at the American Museum of Natural History. Leeds couldn't have imagined that the gig would evolve into a move to Minneapolis and ten years by Prince's side, not to mention a paradigm lifestyle shift for Ms. Gwyn—from the sober world of science to the bawdy world of rock and roll. With the hindsight of a couple decades, the now married couple share two very inside views of their purple years, but often through different sets of eyes.

Alan: Fargnoli sternly warned me to tread lightly until Prince signaled his comfort with having me around. "He takes a minute to warm up to strangers," was Steven's memorable understatement.

I met them in San Diego, direct from a tour with the rock group Kiss. Fargnoli introduced me around. I made a point to befriend the band and bodyguard Chick Huntsberry, who seconded Steve's warning not to bum-rush Prince.

The relationship between an artist and a tour manager is often more personal than one might expect. It's a cliché and a stereotype, but most performers are remarkably insecure. Gaining their confidence means not only demonstrating your skill set but making them like having you around. I didn't worry about the skill set, but becoming "liked" was less tangible. For starters, I needed to learn Prince's backstage rituals and travel preferences. But Chick insisted I not confront him. He said, "If you ask him that stuff, he'll just think you don't know what you're doing."

The Prince dressing room door that Chick protected remained closed until show time. On his way to the stage, Prince paused, shook my hand, and softly mumbled something I couldn't understand. I didn't see him again until we flew to the next town.

KISS had been a coat-and-tie gig; they expected their management in Madison Avenue garb. So the next morning, I showed up at the airport in a conservative pin-striped suit. As I walked the aisle to my seat, I felt like I was on display. Prince never looked up, but Chick nodded. Working

my way back, I locked eyes with a giggling Vanity and Susan Moonsie of Vanity 6, noted a determined disinterest from the Time's Terry Lewis, and then what I took to be a snide glare from Morris Day. Tour promoter Jeff Sharp's expression seemed to say, "I wonder how long this guy is going to last." Everyone was casually dressed, mostly in sweats. It was bad enough being the new guy, but my Madison Avenue shit came off as really pretentious. It was definitely a "what the fuck?" moment for the entire entourage.

Gwen: When Alan called to tell me he had picked up another tour, all it meant was that he wouldn't be home for another month or two. I remembered Alan saying that Prince was going to be the next big thing, but I didn't really know any-

thing about him. Don't misunderstand me, I love music. But when Alan's and my tastes intersected, it took us to concerts by Pat Metheny and Weather Report, not rock stars.

A few months later, Alan was offered a full-time position in Minneapolis. I didn't know how to respond. I guess I just assumed it would break us up. Leaving my job and moving there never occurred to me. All I knew about Minneapolis was that they had a skyway system because it was too cold to walk outside. Guess

"Why do people just stare like they've got nothing else to do?" Prince asked. I didn't dare tell him that if I encountered a pint-sized rock star in high heels, silk pajamas, and a trench coat, I'd probably stare too.

what? Two months later, I quit my job and moved to Minneapolis!

Alan: Once I bought some casual clothes, it didn't take long to get my bearings. It was obviously a tour split into cliques. My responsibilities were Prince and his band. The support acts—the Time and Vanity 6—had their own staffs and agendas. Jimmy Jam Harris and Terry Lewis had famously clashed with Prince over missing a gig, and the Time's morale was forever ruined. Meanwhile, Prince was juggling his relationships with the various girls on the tour. I had assumed he and Vanity were a couple but quickly discovered that their best days were behind them. In fact, Vanity was flirtatious and defiantly self-sufficient. I also learned that Susan Moonsie had once been a

Prince steady and retained a close but apparently platonic friendship with him. Background singer Jill Jones was also around him a lot and I wasn't really sure what that meant.

I didn't try to clock Prince's comings and goings. Even though the group usually flew between cities, whenever it was logistically plausible Prince preferred rolling on his comfy tour bus. His post-show habit was to return to our hotel, shower, and retire to the bus—often spending the nights parked in hotel lots. Chick explained that Prince hated hotel beds, found them all "too hard."

Wherever Prince was and whatever he was doing, if he was happy, then I was happy. But his clandestine ways inevitably aroused suspicion. Where I came from, anyone who worked so hard at privacy usually had something to hide. One night in Oakland, Chick woke me up about 3:00 AM asking for $500 in cash because Prince wanted to take a cruise in his bus. He and whoever was with him had designs of seeing the sunrise over the Golden Gate Bridge. Sounded like an admirably sexy idea to me but $500? I suspected there was a toll to cross the bridge, but I knew it wasn't anywhere near $500! Mind you, in my years as a freelancer, other artists had come for money late at night. And I suspected that those insomniac dollars usually weren't going for anything legal. So it took a couple days before the band could convince me that this weird, secretive guy wasn't a full-blown junkie. Of course, he was anything but—back then he seldom even drank. By rock-and-roll tour standards, the *1999* gang was pretty "clean." There were no heavy cokeheads or stoners, just the occasional spliff wafting down hotel hallways.

A few months after the tour, I was offered a full-time position in Minneapolis, Prince's hometown, as a management liaison or, as the West Coast–based Fargnoli put it, "an off-road road manager." I didn't really want to leave Gwen or New York, but it was an alluring opportunity. Prince was fine-tuning the script to *Purple Rain*. It was bound to be an interesting ride.

By the time filming began, Gwen had joined me. Prince seemed to accept her rather quickly. We'd even double-date to a movie with him and Susan Moonsie, ending up at his now infamous purple house in suburban Chanhassen watching videos or checking out his newest songs. Sometimes, he would quietly sit at his piano and just start to play. Even in such a casual setting those moments could be spellbinding.

Gwen: When I got to Minneapolis, they were rehearsing the *Purple Rain* concert scenes. When Alan introduced me to Prince, he shook my hand, very formally. I really didn't know what to make of him. He didn't act like anybody I'd ever met before. He seldom talked, so you never knew where he stood or where you stood with him. I always caught myself looking at him, trying to read him. Later, on tour, that backfired when one of my responsibilities was to manage the media photographers allowed to shoot five minutes of the show from the pit in front of the stage. I had to accompany them to make certain they didn't wander off and shoot something else behind our backs. Of course, it was an awesome perspective of the action, literally right below Prince's feet. One day, he sent word that I needed to conceal myself down there. He told Alan, "How does Gwen expect me to stay in my zone onstage if I look down and see her familiar face starin' up at me?"

I wasn't used to having to tiptoe around someone. I was shocked by how many people were willing to do that— band members, crew, security, even Prince's own family. And I wasn't the only one who felt that way. My first friend in Minneapolis was Susan Moonsie. She had a solid family background and strong values. Susan's head was screwed on right; she knew who she was. Amidst all the craziness, she didn't define herself through Vanity 6 or her relationship with Prince. I respected her.

Before there was a Paisley Park, Prince didn't really have an office or a staff other than Chick and Sandy, his personal assistant. The living room in our apartment became the company office by default. People were coming and going, signing contracts, picking up checks

(*right*) Prince, circa summer of 1982.
An alternate shot appears on the
7-inch cover of "Delirious."
Photo by Allen Beaulieu.

or per diems. As Alan's load got heavier, Prince started asking me to do things, and I ended up on payroll. Like any new employee, I wanted to make a good impression, please the boss. But I quickly learned that no matter how far you went above and beyond the call of duty, Prince wasn't one to applaud your efforts. Everything had to be a slam dunk. It wasn't real to me. Because in real life, everything isn't a slam dunk. Sometimes, though, he would do stuff that just had you scratching your head. Early one morning, our phone rang and it was Prince. When he called, he never made small talk, not even a hello. Usually it was just, "Alan there?" But this time, he said, "Gwen, do you know what time it is?"

I stumbled for a second, looked at a clock, and told him the time. To which he responded, "Okay, you passed." Click.

I passed? I chuckled. Whenever I got glimpses of Prince's humanity, it was reassuring. Then I could tell myself he has a heart. I needed to be reminded of that, because he tried so hard to hide it. But I instantly respected his talent and his tireless work ethic. I'd never seen anything like it.

Alan: The huge impact of *Purple Rain* was somewhat unexpected, except by Prince. He didn't seem surprised by reports of audiences reacting to the movie like it was a live concert. The first time most of us saw the film in a real theater was the glitzy premiere in Hollywood. But that audience was mostly blasé industry folks. The next day, Prince woke up and said he wanted to see a screening at a neighborhood theater in Westwood. He knew the only way to witness a real audience was to disguise himself. One of our security guys went to the theater to reserve the back row, explaining that we would sneak in after the film had begun. Meanwhile, Prince's stylists, the late Earl Jones and Robyn Lynch, hooked him up. His hair was stuffed under a hat, and Jones added a theatrical moustache. Prince wore eyeglasses and an uncharacteristically ordinary wardrobe that had been hastily purchased on Melrose Avenue. To test the disguise, he called Gwen and asked her

to meet us in the lobby without revealing what we were up to. She did, and soon Prince walked out of the elevator and sat down across from her. She didn't recognize him until he said something. She should have said, "You passed."

So off we went. Other than the theater manager and the kids working the refreshment stand, nobody knew we were there. I thought he had been spotted a few minutes into the film until I realized the kids were shrieking at the screen. It was insane. You could barely hear the dialogue. A couple folks recognized him when we got up to leave, but we were gone before the word could spread.

Gwen: Earl Jones and I planned to bust them—meet them at the theater as they were leaving and holler, "Look, there's Prince!" But on our way there, they passed us. We were too late.

Things got crazy for Prince at home too. Fans had discovered his house. It wasn't anything over the top, just a nice home on a generous lot, except the house was painted purple! Thankfully, it sat about fifty yards back from the street. The lot was fenced and there was an electronic gate across the driveway. Prince was in and out of town a lot, so the house often sat vacant. After an attempted break-in, it was decided someone should house-sit when he was away. Since Alan usually traveled with him, I became one of the occasional house sitters. One day I was there, killing time doing laundry, when I glimpsed at the closed-circuit video/intercom and spotted six or seven fans congregated at the front gate. I was curious, so I hit the button to hear what they were saying. But I must have hit the wrong button, because suddenly I could see the gate opening on the monitor. I frantically tried every button on the wall but nothing stopped the gate. The fans whose faces I could make out on the screen were awestruck. Then sure enough, as if they had been directed by a higher power, they cautiously proceeded past the gate and up the driveway towards the house. They were like the walking dead! I freaked out for a second, but I knew I had to do something, so I

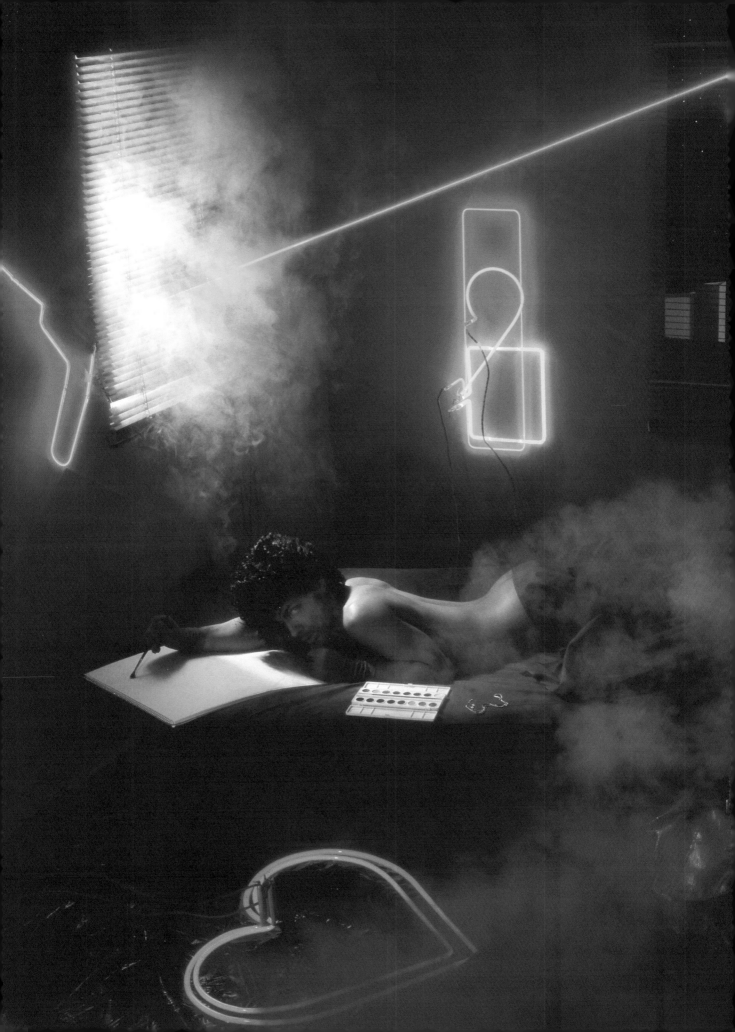

(*left*) Prince, circa summer of 1982.
Photo by Allen Beaulieu.

decided that the best defense is a good offense. I ran out to head them off before they could either scatter or get to the front door. Then I acted like I had let them in on purpose. They were overwhelmed with gratitude! I explained that Prince was out of town and then gave them a quick, impromptu tour around the grounds, told them about the lake in the back, and finally said they had to go. I just prayed that Prince would never find out.

Alan: After *Purple Rain*, we all had to adjust to the hysteria that greeted Prince everywhere he went. He pretty much welcomed the adoration, but there were times when it threw him. Before he blew up, Prince would comfortably frequent First Avenue [club in Minneapolis], particularly on Fridays when girl watching was at its best. Then one night, Prince, Chick, Jerome Benton, and I met at the club and were just kind of loafing in the dark near the back of the dance floor when we were suddenly surrounded by gawking fans. Struggling to maintain his cool, Prince leaned towards my ear and said, "Why do people just stare like they've got nothing else to do?" I didn't dare tell him that if I encountered a pint-sized rock star in high heels, silk pajamas, and a trench coat, I'd probably stare too.

Gwen: One of the good things about working for Prince was that he only liked having people around him that he was comfortable with. He was completely okay with me going on the *Purple Rain* tour as Alan's assistant. Since the alternative was being home alone for six months, I was grateful for the opportunity. Alan had been out there all his life with major stars like James Brown or KISS, but touring with a rock star was unlike anything I had ever been part of. I quickly realized that a lot of people "in the business" were also glorified groupies. But I was never smitten with celebrities. I had known people like Hugh Masekela, D.T. of Kool and the Gang, and Claude Cave from Mandrill, but they were social friends. I had nothing to do with their professional lives. This was a radically different world, a cultish insular existence in which it was easy to lose track of what day it was or what city you were in. And the excess and lack of accountability was mind-blowing. I had come from a museum, a not-for-profit institution where every postage stamp was accounted for. But here, everything was sent by FedEx or even more expensively, airlines counter-to-counter. Prince couldn't seem to wait for anything.

Over the years, I grew eternally grateful for the experiences I had because of Prince—the friends I made and the places I'd seen. It became intoxicating; you couldn't help but change or you'd get left behind. But I never understood the degree of influence a rock star could accumulate and never got used to seeing adults act stupidly. Prince, his employees, his fans, managers, promoters, agents, producers—it was all a fascinating study in psychology.

Alan: It was great having Gwen on the road, but it took a little adjustment. The road rat in me wasn't used to rolling in tandem, and at first, she was a duck out of water. The fact that the Prince posse was so inbred helped. We all already knew each other. The Revolution's Bobby Z, Wendy Melvoin, and Lisa Coleman each had siblings who were part of the extended family. Even my own saxophonist brother Eric eventually came aboard, augmenting Prince's band.

Prince's father, pianist John Nelson, was another familiar face. He already enjoyed casual friendships with many of us including Gwen. Father and son couldn't boast of a warm, fuzzy history, but Prince seemed bent on making up for lost time. John attended all of his son's major events and sure didn't mind his entrée to rock-star creature comforts, including the companionship of a cutie who had been a popular *Playboy* model. One of his visits was to our New Orleans show at the Superdome.

I was in the production office, which happened to be located completely across the stadium from the star dressing room, when my radio (walkie-talkie) buzzed. It was Bobby Z, and he sounded ominous: "Alan, you better get over here."

I was confused. It was showtime—I should have been meeting the band at the stage. "No, put it on hold and get over here. Prince and Gwen are about to go at it."

I had absolutely no idea what he was talking about, but I sure didn't like the sound of it. The price of having Gwen on the road was anxiety over what might happen if Prince's star shit ever pushed her buttons just a little too far.

Alan: Bobby Z assumed he had stumbled upon the start of something rather than the finish, which explains his radio heads-up. But it was over—an insignificant incident in the scheme of things. Gwen had run into what every rock star employee does at some point: the always-lurking sense of entitlement that our culture indulges on celebrities. There is inevitably a moment, an unexpected issue, an odd scenario that serves to emphasize that every show has a star, and we're not it. With Prince, those moments usually surfaced

sports cars.

On the creative tip, *Purple Rain* was Prince's most ambitious road production yet. Cleverly recreating many of the performance scenes in the film was a blessing and a curse. The heavily scripted show meant strictly regimented lighting and production cues and left little room for musical spontaneity. Other than Prince's mid-show piano medley and the encore jam, the show was pretty much identical from night to night. I could set my watch by what song they were playing. But every fresh audience was pandemonium from the first note to the last.

Our crack technical crew was as professional and efficient as the performers. Still, every tour has that one Murphy's Law day where everything that can go wrong does go wrong. Ours was a one-off in Birmingham, Alabama. Ironically, it was the one gig without our production manager Tom Marzullo who was away advancing venues for future shows. His absence hadn't worried me; our stage manager was top drawer, and by then, the production was almost on automatic pilot. But so much went wrong that I later teased Marzullo that he had paid someone to sabotage the show so he'd be missed.

Purple Rain was Prince's most ambitious road production yet. Cleverly recreating many of the performance scenes in the film was a blessing and a curse. But every fresh audience was pandemonium from the first note to the last.

Gwen: It was just before showtime when I ran into John Nelson standing outside Prince's dressing room. Naturally, we greeted each other and struck up a conversation. Suddenly, Prince emerged. As usual, no hello, just, "My dad is like me; he doesn't like to talk."

In other words, leave him the hell alone! I was crushed. Maybe Prince didn't realize how friendly John and I had become back home, but here were two adults having a very normal conversation and being scolded like kids. I was humiliated, and I didn't know how to take it. John clammed up, so I lashed back the only smart-ass way I knew how and muttered something like, "He didn't seem to mind talking until you came out."

Just then, the band showed up for their preshow prayer ritual with the boss.

when he was nervous or bothered about something totally unrelated. In this case, he was simply trying to preserve his backstory, a mystique about his father to equal his own.

Despite these little bumps in the road, the *Purple Rain* tour developed a rhythm. All the shows sold out as quickly as tickets could be printed—record-breaking multi-show runs in L.A., San Francisco, Detroit, D.C., Philadelphia, Chicago, and New York. When we landed in a major city, we moved in with purpose. It was some sort of quasi-decadent invasion—sex, drugs, and rock and roll. And fast cars. An L.A. newspaper even published a story about a shortage of luxury rentals in Beverly Hills, because almost everyone in our group opted to spend the week rolling in our own spiffy, high-end

Gwen: Before that Birmingham show, all we were worried about was the weather. An ice storm was cooking, threatening the highways and airports between us and our next stop in Memphis. We had chartered a Delta 727 for the band and crew, but, as usual, Prince planned to ride his bus. When you put the whole entourage together after a show, almost a hundred people, we could be a pretty boisterous bunch. Prince hated those flights.

Alan: Prince's driver was pacing about, suggesting that he really should be leaving early with an empty bus to avoid getting stranded by the storm. We debated that wisdom, knowing that Prince would disapprove. The one thing we all agreed on was not to tell him anything until we made a final decision. As Chick had taught me, Prince would just think we weren't sure of what we were doing. (Of course, if

he didn't like our decision later, he'd think that anyhow.)

Showtime. And suddenly the weather was the least of our problems. The set typically began with what's called a "reveal," the band in silhouette, behind a curtain that dramatically disappeared at the downbeat of "Let's Go Crazy." The downbeat came but the curtain didn't. The curtain mechanism stalled about knee high off the stage. The song was nearly over before the crew finished manually (and clumsily) gathering the bulk over the truss above.

Little did we know, our night from hell was just beginning. Later in the show, Prince had a quick change after which he reemerged via a hydraulic lift for "Darling Nikki." First, Prince bumped his head under the stage climbing onto the lift. Then, the song started and once again mechanics failed...this time with just the top of his sore cranium protruding into the audience sight lines. It looked like a cantaloupe laying on the stage. Finally, a couple crew guys pushed him the rest of the way up. He was not happy.

The mishaps understandably escalated the tension backstage. But by the encore, our attention was back to the weather. Reports were that sections of U.S. 78 between Birmingham and Memphis were icing up and threatening to close. We would have to hightail it to the airport with hopes our plane could get off before the storm reached the 'Ham. And while the idea of Prince flying with us after this raggedy show was downright ugly, we had no choice. Worse yet, the band and crew had checked out of our hotel before the show, but Prince had not. We'd have to wait for him to shower and pack up.

As it turned out, there was a storm of another kind about to strike. The (literal) climax of the show was Prince climbing atop huge P.A. stacks where he'd grab a prop guitar rigged to mimic an orgasm by forcefully shooting harmless soapsuds well into the front rows. Sure enough, in the spirit of the entire night, when it came time to shoot his load, Prince's Viagra-starved guitar failed and limply dripped jism to the stage.

Prince stalked towards his waiting limo. With Tom Marzullo nowhere around to catch the blame, I seriously wondered if I still had a job. But I had to act as if I did—we had a show in Memphis to worry about.

Gwen: Prince typically fled the venue before house lights were on. Now, if this was the real world, one would grab Prince and explain the situation. But this was the purple world where nothing was real anymore. And this night of all nights, Chick wasn't about to allow anyone to intercept them. We could only assume he would tell Prince about the storm on the way to the hotel. But before their car was out of the arena, Chick was on the radio. "Tell Alan, Prince says he needs to be at his hotel room before anybody goes anywhere."

It must have been the fastest load-out of the entire tour. In less than an hour, we were on a chartered bus headed to the hotel. We had spoken to the airport and were warned not to dawdle. Once the ice storm began, they would close the runways, and we'd be stuck. But we had no choice but to wait in the clammy bus while Alan faced Prince. A lot of us felt badly that Alan was the only one catching hell, but the bigger picture was we had to get out of there with some quickness. Everyone was tired and on edge, particularly the fragile flyers like Wendy and Lisa.

Alan: The bus felt like a funeral home, everyone knew what I was in for, and I'd like to think some of the techs felt a bit guilty, since I was really taking one for the team. I went to Prince's suite and knocked on the door. He opened it, turned his back and stalked towards a large dining room table pointing for me to sit down. For a few minutes—which seemed like hours—he just glared and said nothing. Finally, he snapped, "What can you tell me so that I know none of this is going to happen again?"

I went through each fuck-up, one by one, offering rather technical explanations of what had gone wrong and what we intended to do to prevent any repeats.

He wasn't convinced. Neither was I, really. Life isn't perfect. Shit happens. And the opening curtain bit had been shaky long before Birmingham. The quiet in the room was stagnant. Then I realized that Prince was still in his stage clothes. He hadn't even showered. So I gulped and changed the subject. Chick hadn't said a word about the storm, the bus, or the flight. (Thanks a bunch, Chick.) On top of everything, now I had to explain that Prince's fancy of a leisurely night on his bus was a wrap or he risked blowing the next show. Somehow, we landed in icy Memphis about four in the morning. Prince was silent the whole way.

All it meant to me was what I'd known for years. Life on the road was always an adventure. And since I still had a job, I guess I could finally assume that I had succeeded in making him like having me around. After all, he had fired others for much less.

Several years later, he once asked me why I thought he was under-appreciated as a guitarist. I foolishly suggested that he should consider a brief tour of elite concert venues concentrating solely on his musicianship, performing without his usual bells and whistles, even to the point of dressing down, perhaps in blue jeans and a turtleneck. Dripping with sarcasm, his patronizing response was, "What? And look like you?" Maybe he didn't like having me around after all. (In 2002, he did just such a tour, all except for the jeans and turtle neck.)

Purple Rain led my way to four more world tours, countless award shows and special events, and then three years of running Prince's Paisley Park Records. I had the privilege of watching the evolution of one of the most talented and influential pop stars ever. In such a heady atmosphere, it was inevitable that Prince would grow, the company would grow, things would become more complicated, and relationships would change. All of that happened, usually for the better. But I've always wondered if there's any tiny part of Prince that ever yearns for those exciting simpler years. The fact is, we all passed! ⬤

SOUL
CALIBER
Frank Ocean

by **Matthew Trammell**

After focusing on a songwriting career, Frank Ocean switched his sights to singing for the masses. His free download album, *Nostalgia, Ultra*, became an instant Internet sensation for its personal, thoughtful take on modern R&B. Now Frank finds himself in a unique position of calling the shots and taking his time on his forthcoming major-label debut.

Luckily, Frank Ocean's throat is feeling better. It's a few days after his aborted New York City debut, and his voice arrives full and deep over the phone, with no sign of the sore tonsils that devastated a line of ticket-holders that frigid Sunday night. After announcing that his show was canceled, he posted on his Tumblr page: "im really sorry yall. i'll be back soon as i'm healthy. thats my word."

It's a word fans have learned to cherish, for Frank Ocean is a man of few of them. When he posted his debut album, *Nostalgia, Ultra*, for free download in February 2011, he offered just a pun on his blog: "[frank]: my arms are tired. [gurl]: drop your album." The link was given a viral boost when his Odd Future–affiliate Tyler, the Creator re-posted it at the peak of his own Internet hype: "Smooth Ass Music About Bitches, Relationships And Being A Rich Young Nigga…But In A Swagged Out Way," he wrote of the project. Up until then, members of Odd Future, the L.A. collective of rappers, producers, skaters, and vandals, were most known for their vitriol-drenched rhymes and edgy, gory music videos—they were also critical darlings, and any output from the crew was met with feverish attention amongst press, artists, and fans alike. After being ignored by his label Def Jam for almost two years (the A&R that signed him in 2009 quit soon after, a common industry hiccup that leaves artists in limbo), it seemed that a few tastemaker tweets was all he'd needed: Frank Ocean went from a bookmarked link to a critically acclaimed, genre-smashing phenomenon in as quickly as it took the twenty-three-year-old to hit "publish." The label quickly released a couple singles on iTunes and scrambled to package a commercial release of the album, but sample issues and runaway hype ultimately bested a corporate co-opting of his brand. The official release of *Nostalgia, Ultra* has been scrapped in favor of a new, upcoming release.

Ocean's lips stayed tight as praise and adoration flew his way from all corners of the music universe: *Nostalgia*'s witty, dense songwriting, eclectic production, and cohesive personality exhilarated what had been a largely dormant R&B landscape. He

interpolated the Eagles, Coldplay, MGMT. He sang about swing-sets, gay marriage, Coachella, heartbreak, sports cars, ambition, Islam, his father. He'd come up as a songwriter, penning deep album cuts for Brandy, John Legend, and Justin Bieber. He was older than the rest of the teenaged Odd Future hooligans, and hailed from Louisiana as opposed to L.A. Today, Ocean has established himself as one of music's hottest commodities, penning songs for Beyoncé and landing two features on Jay-Z and Kanye West's mammoth *Watch the Throne*. But much about the young artist remained a mystery—so when he literally vanished moments before he was set to hit the Bowery Ballroom stage, it felt at once calculated and vindicating: buy tickets, stand on line, and see a show? Frank Ocean would never make it that easy.

A few questions have been answered since he arrived, but Ocean remains one of the most elusive emerging artists in recent memory. During our two-hour conversation, he opens up for the first time ever about growing up in New Orleans, his formative years as an artist, the recording and promoting of his first album, and the complex personal life that has inspired such a remarkable career.

Can you paint a general portrait of what it was like growing up in New Orleans? The culture and music of the city are renowned across the nation. What are some of your earliest memories?

Shit… I remember the first flood I ever experienced. I was little, maybe like six. It flooded probably two inches underneath the threshold of our door, so it didn't get in the house. All the houses in New Orleans are raised off the ground because of floods and shit. So it was like three feet of water. My cousins and I stacked up milk crates and were using it as a diving board into the floodwaters. We were doing that all day until one of my neighbors came out there on a little swamp-style boat, and grabbed a water moccasin out of the water and cut its head off against the fence. That was the last time I swam in any floodwaters. I think that was my earliest memory of something that was really a part of New Orleans culture. I consider hurricanes to be a part of New

Orleans culture in a weird way.

You were in New Orleans for Hurricane Katrina. Did you and your family lose a lot when it hit?

Nah. I was in college, and my dorm was fifteen stories, so I was up towards the top, but the whole bottom levels were molded up, so I couldn't go in my dorm for months. My mom had just built a home on the West Bank, which is on the west side of the Mississippi River. That side of the town didn't get as much water as the Ninth Ward and the neighborhoods that I grew up in, by the Seventh Ward. Just to put it in perspective: the house I grew up in got eight feet of water, and the house we moved into got a little bit of roof damage. We made it out all right.

We haven't had many contemporary artists who've grown up in New Orleans and brought those experiences directly into their music. Lil Wayne has touched on it a bit before, but not many others. Do you feel that experiencing Katrina has informed your creativity since then?

I can't credit it with too much. I can credit it with being the reason I moved to L.A. Ultimately, the reason I'm successful might be attributed to Katrina. I don't think I would've moved if it hadn't been for that storm, and I don't think I'd have been successful if I stayed in New Orleans.

You've known that you wanted to be a recording artist since you were about twelve years old. What was your musical context when you decided you wanted to be a part of the music industry?

At twelve, thirteen, I was obsessed with the *Billboard* charts. I had a friend who I grew up with, my homie Chico; he and I would really look at those charts all the time and predict what songs would move up and how many positions. I would listen to those songs more for sport, and I would listen to stuff my mom played in the car. She would always listen to Toni Braxton. Then it was Phyllis Hyman and fuckin' Celine Dion, who I loved, Whitney Houston, Mariah Carey, Anita Baker—a bunch of females. Sometimes, she would weird out and listen to the *Phantom of the Opera*

soundtrack, seriously.

By the time I started buying records on my own, I had signed up for the BMG CD catalog. The first record I ever bought was *The Marshall Mathers LP*, which kind of peels your wig back at that age, like, "Whoa, what the fuck is this?" That really inspired my interest in hip-hop and rap music. I was always a little picky when it came to rappers, because I started with Em. He's so fucking good that you kind of develop a little bit of snobbery as a teenager about the rappers you listen to.

That seems really common in our generation of music lovers. Eminem was the first artist that really exhilarated us.
Right, right. That was the first real album I ever listened to with that kind of content. It definitely fucked me up. Also, being a singer, and around that time starting to really believe in myself as a singer-songwriter, I had a thing for voices. I started getting into more of the guys that were singing: Donny Hathaway, Sam Cooke, a little bit of Stevie, and definitely got into Prince. I used to listen to Michael Bolton's greatest hits and cover albums. I'd listen to any voice that I was drawn to. I'd listen to it as close as I could.

Prince is very evident in your music, as is Stevie. Would you consider some of those voices ones that you aspire to or try to emulate?
Trying to get as many colors out of your voice is something I learned from the singers I mentioned, like Donny, for example. Just how it goes from being so rich to so broken. Prince can almost give you any color. He was so fearless with his expression. He could be effeminate, like when he did that female persona, Camille. I used to love to listen to Mariah or Celine, where they'd go to the top of their range and the tone would disappear. I don't know how to describe it, but I've asked mix engineers, and they call it "the sparkle"—it'll sparkle at the top.

Right, it almost ceases to be a voice with tone, and it's just a pitch that's as sharp as a thin piece of string.
Exactly, exactly. Even to this day, it's voice

I prefer over any instrument. Voice, and then guitar, because it sounds like a voice to me.

It's not very common for a thirteen-year-old to know they want to be a songwriter instead of a performer. What drew you to songwriting as opposed to just trying to be a singer initially?
My skill for writing preexisted my skills in music. I knew that I enjoyed writing before I knew that I enjoyed singing and performing music. As a kid, if my mom and I got into it, we would write each other letters. I'm talking about a six-, seven-, eight-year-old writing letters to his mom about why he thinks his punishment is unjust, or why he doesn't want to go to school in the morning, or why she has to go to work in the morning and come home so late. I didn't get to creative writing until I was a little bit older. I wrote three fully bound little books—I think my mom still has them at home. When you're a kid, you don't have an idea of structure, you're just writing whenever you want to write. The only reason I wrote those books is because I was in a gifted class in elementary, and I overextended myself and wrote more than I had to for some projects.

What were some of your first records about? Do you remember any of your earliest songs?
I remember my first rhyme. The first song I wrote was probably a rap. I was young, all right? I'll put the disclaimer on it. I was nine. My rhyme was: "I went to the park, it was so dark / A nigga tried to rob me with a spoon and a fork / He put the spoon to my head, a gun to my leg / The nigga didn't know I had a razor blade / He took all my money, and all my jewelry / I said, 'Look, fake nigga, I'm tired of you…'" and I don't remember the rest. [*laughs*] That was my first rhyme.

Was that drawn from a real-life experience?
Nah, hell nah. I was just trying to be cool.

I'm not going to lie to you. That may be the first one, but we still get that Frank Ocean imagery. I saw the park. The traces of it were there.

[*laughs*] Yeah, man, you know, it was a diamond in the rough, I guess.

You got your first placement and really started getting serious with the Midi Mafia, right?
I got my first placement with an old friend, one of my first friends in the music business when I moved to L.A., this producer named Bryan Kennedy. I was at his home studio in Burbank, and we were just hanging out, writing and shit. An artist from Epic named Noel Gourdin came by the studio, and we wrote a song called "I Fell," and it wound up being on his album [*After My Time*]. After that, I wrote a song with Bryan Kennedy at the Record Plant in L.A. at some sort of writing camp. It was a song called "Locket." The A&R for Brandy's album heard it and loved it. She called a meeting and asked if me, Bryan Kennedy, and a couple other writers could just write her whole album. They put me on this $2,500-a-month retainer to come to the studio and write songs for Brandy's album. So we were working out of Paramount and a few other studios. This was about eight to ten months before the *Human* album dropped. That was my first time really being with an artist, where the artist was in the studio, and we were working closely. I developed a relationship with Brandy. It was through her that I met Midi Mafia.

Towards the end of that, the A&R really fucked all of us over. We'd been working for months and really doing incredible shit, and she fucked us over and did a song deal with Rodney Jerkins. He basically—and I don't mind saying this—he basically just listened to the songs that we were doing and attempted to recreate that sound, and made the album. The A&R told me that one of my songs, "1st & Love," was on it, and none of the other ones were making it. It was my first real disappointment in the music business, kind of a right of passage, I guess.

When you started recording *Nostalgia, Ultra*, you were signed to Def Jam but didn't have much label support. What was that recording process like? Who were some of the first people you reached out to?
For one, I knew I had to secure a studio. That was one of the most daunting tasks,

Photo by Julian Berman.

apart from getting beats and shit. I had to find an engineer to record me and track me, because I'm not that awesome at Pro Tools. For beats, I reached out to, obviously, Hit-Boy, I reached out to Tricky [Stewart], Midi Mafia, Chase N. Cashe. I reached out to Brandy for backgrounds. I wanted it to have a cohesive sound, so I tried to pick beats that went well together. I busted my ass trying to get the sequence to ride a certain sort of way. I picked samples partly based on what I liked and partly on what was available. I lucked up with the Eagles fully hi-fi instrumental; I didn't think I was even going to find that. The studio I was at didn't have the vocal chain that I wanted, so I was renting shit just to give it a sound. I wanted it to sound like the shit in stores; I didn't want it to sound like a mixtape. It wasn't a mixtape to me; it was an album just as much as any other release was—it just wasn't in the major-label system. So I treated it like that, I A&R'd it like that, I recorded it and mixed it like that. I spent time and money on the mixes. I didn't have a lot of money to be spending racks on mixing it. So it was definitely a labor of love and a passion. It just had to get done, as far as I was concerned. It was the only way that I could be heard in the way that I wanted to be heard.

Did you anticipate the overwhelming critical reception it got? Did you feel the potency of the material when you were recording it?
I felt that the body of work was strong. I felt that it was the best work I had done so far. And I felt that it displayed my talents accurately. But I was still so shocked. Famous people that I didn't really know were telling me how awesome it was. You're still in a haze of disbelief for a little while before it settles in, like, "Wow, this is really happening. People are really fucking with this thing, and this thing is you." It's not contrived.

To be honest with you, I thought I'd have to throw some block parties in East L.A. and play the shit at parties and shit and get people hyped on it. I was thinking of marketing ploys, tasteful marketing ploys, to even attract attention to it. I wasn't thinking I could just put it on my Tumblr and put my hands in the air...

[*laughs*] And just have the rest be history. You've shot videos for "Novacane" and "Swim Good." Did you know those would be breakout singles?
I didn't want "Novacane" or "Swim Good" to be the single. I don't like that term. Maybe because I don't like the radio, and I don't think anybody else does. It's like a conveyor belt with little soul. When I think of single, I automatically picture putting something that I've put everything into on some conveyor belt. It becomes way more about science, about feelings and shit. Apart from that, if I had to take a single off of there and had to use that conveyor belt for one of my shits, I would have probably went with... I don't know. That's a good question.

What does it then say to you that a song as dark and arcane as "Novacane" is a breakout track that people flocked to? Does that change your thinking at all?
No, it doesn't, because "Novacane" wasn't a successful pop song. I knew that it wouldn't be a successful pop song. It was successful in pop culture, but it wasn't successful on *Billboard* Hot 100. It wasn't built for that. There was no way I could see that record being number one. In my spirit, I always knew that it wasn't that record. I'm actually glad that it wasn't, because it's true to form. It's an important song for my career, for sure. "Novacane" pulled people down the wormhole hopefully into my space of music, and I think there's a lot more there. And there might be some shit for the *Billboard* Hot 100 in my catalog somewhere.

The material you contributed to *Watch the Throne* was very politically and socially aware. Would you say "Made in America" is an accurate portrayal of some of the social and political beliefs that you hold?
Yeah. I don't think of myself like a super political guy. I don't think there's that much commentary on "Made in America." When I was writing that song, I was trying to be humorous—most people don't get my sense of humor. It was like, "Sweet King Martin, sweet Queen Coretta," all these Black figures, "sweet Baby Jesus," the Black baby Jesus. I was thinking about how, after all that we've suffered through, niggas think I've made it in America if I'm driving a

Phantom, or if my chain is VVS, or if I'm at the club spending racks on bitches exposing themselves to me.

It seems like Jay-Z and Kanye were somewhat in on that joke. Their verses aren't necessarily about pro-Black themes. Kanye spends most of his verse talking about fashion. That materialism idea is being toyed with throughout the song.
Right. It's interesting to me to think what those figures would have thought about our definition of "making it" now. "No Church in the Wild," that's a different thing. It's a commentary on hierarchy and how people lay themselves out. An atheist can be more powerful than the Pope, by state of mind, just because he doesn't believe in anything higher than himself. That song was a little deeper. There was no humor there; that was pretty serious. I guess, it's political, I don't know. Jay and Kanye played me what they were doing, and I knew what I needed to say. It's one thing being in a room with your heroes making music and just tripping off that. But to be in a room with your heroes doing something that they actually fuck with and are giving you props for, that's extra special.

It had to have been a crazy experience to come into the project after they'd already been working on it, and then ending up getting the first track on the album.
That was a big deal to me. I'm not too proud to say it—that meant a lot. Definitely a shining moment.

R&B has always been a controversial and malleable musical category. It's gone from rock and roll, to bebop, to funk, to soul, to pop. Now, anytime you have a Black vocalist saying, "Ooh, baby, I love you," that's R&B. Artists like Jamie XX or Adele or Amy Winehouse don't get labeled as just R&B. Are you fighting against that stigma?
I hope that I help to at least start that conversation, about why, if a Black guy walks up to you and says that he sings, you immediately say that he's an R&B singer. I don't think it's accurate. I mean, what is all that shit? Like, what do genres mean? How are they distinguished? Chord progressions? I know there's a blues scale—I don't know.

You went from inching into the songwriting world and putting out this debut album, and in a few months you're working with Beyoncé, Jay-Z, and Kanye West. Is there anyone else out there that you would want to write for? Where do you go from here as a songwriter?

I'd love to write a verse or a chorus or something on Earl's album when he gets back. I'd love to work with—

I'm sorry to interrupt. But you know you just said something really important. We are to be expecting an album from Earl Sweatshirt when he comes back?

[*laughs*] Don't take my word for it. You have to ask one of the presidents of Odd Future Records for an official statement on that. I'd imagine he might be itching to record an LP when he gets back, but what do I know?

So Earl is an artist on Odd Future Records, is that what that means?

That didn't mean anything other than what I said.

You've mentioned that you spoke to Tyler on the phone for about two hours before you ever met him. What was that conversation about?

You know Tyler. It was all over the place. He let me know that he was just about to jack off before I called him. That was our first exchange. From there, we talked about music, dinosaurs, the Grammys he wanted and I wanted. It was just creative people talking about what drives them and what pops up in the head. From the first conversation, I had a sense that he was on to something.

On the song "There Will Be Tears," you sing a bit about your father's absence from your life. What exactly is your history with him?

That song is about my grandfather, who stepped in more as a father than my biological father. The last time I saw my father, he took me to the department store and bought me a pocketknife. I never saw him again. I was, like, six. Prior to the pocketknife department-store shopping spree, I didn't see him much anyways. I didn't have

any relationship with him. If he walked into this room I'm sitting in right now, I wouldn't know it's him. I don't know what he looks like. I lost my grandfather early too, but he was around long enough for me to at least learn a few things about being a man.

Much of your music is aimed at women, and reckons with womanhood and relationships. How has your relationship with your mother, and lack of one with your father, informed how you write about women and how you think about them?

I have a tremendous amount of respect for women because of my mother. When you have a child, women have to step up to the plate quicker than a man. I respect her for that. It's not a small job. I know for my mom, especially as bad as I was during school and adolescence and shit, I put her through hell, and her love for me never wavered. The same can't be said about my father. I look at women through that lens. I have a deep compassion for all people, and that compassion comes from my mom.

You've mentioned you didn't want to bring too many big-name artists onto your next album. You said specifically that you wanted to do it without a feature from Kanye. Who are some of the people that we can expect you to be working with, and what's the direction you'll be taking?

I'm expanding sonically, I hope. I'm working with one guy, this guy Molay. I worked for a weekend at the Record Plant in L.A. with Pharrell, and we did a couple songs that will most likely be on it. I did "Disillusioned" with this keyboardist, but it's not finished yet. I'll probably finish that up with Tricky Stewart. It's sample free, but there is an Elton John "Bennie and the Jets" interpolation, and there's a Mary J. Blige interpolation as well. The sound—it's a whole lot of synths and a whole lot of rhythm.

Judging by "Disillusioned" and "Super Rich Kids," they both have an '80s, synth-heavy Prince feel to them. Is that the general direction of the next album?

Like I said, down the rabbit hole. There's a

few more places that we go on this album. "Super Rich Kids" is the tentative title. I'm bouncing a few ideas around for others, like "Hilfiger Nigga." It's expanding on a lot of the shit that I did on *Nostalgia*, for sure. The song structures, the production, the story-telling. Still very visual.

Is the label more hands-on with this project? Do you still have the space to function as independently as you did with the first album?

I function as independently as I did—it's in better studios. My recording conditions are a little bit more posh, but it's the same. I still don't have an A&R; I'm holding all the creative control. I'm making the record that I want to make.

Probably a nicer budget this time around?

Yeah, man. Definitely a cool budget. Trying not to go over, still be cost-effective. Definitely more resources: I can call in a harp section or a string section or whatever.

You mentioned that you don't make beats, but you're hands-on with the production of the record in the classic sense?

Very much so. I'm in everybody's Kool-Aid, all the producers I work with. Not micromanaging—I like people to be creative and invested if I decide to work with them. But I definitely oversee things and get my hands dirty. Brainstorming things for instrumental arrangements, and obviously composing vocal arrangements alongside whoever I'm with. I keep to a small crew of people. The whole record is done by Molay, Pharrell, and Tricky. So I'm there, man. If at three minutes and ten seconds in a song, there needs to be a horn quartet that comes in for seven seconds and never shows up again, that idea is probably coming from me.

When can we expect to hear or see something?

Eh, whenever it's done. I don't know the timeline; I'm pretty anti-release date. It's going to be different on this one, for sure. It'll be much more structured this time around. You might get a warning that's a little bit more than five minutes before, only because it has to be. ◐

HOME GROWN

Toro y Moi

by **Matthew Trammell**
photography **Robert Adam Mayer**

Chaz Bundick began his journey as Toro
y Moi creating shoegazing bedroom
electro. But by getting back to basics
and playing his instruments live, he has
opened a doorway into lush and melodic
R&B grooves, transcending any previously
ascribed tags.

Chaz Bundick never thought he'd be the subject of an interview. The unassuming, bespectacled Southern gentleman did not presume a life in the spotlight, and still doesn't—he's a quiet guy from a quiet town with a quiet degree in graphic design. As we sit in the balcony of New York City's Webster Hall, hours before he is set to hit the stage, Bundick speaks in quick, scattered sentences, words shrinking into his chin as he struggles for the point he always offers but never insists upon. He peers over the railing more than once to take in the empty venue as the opening act sound-checks: "Man, that stage is huge," he murmurs, making no attempt to downplay his preshow jitters. His unkempt hair, relaxed T-shirts, and racially ambiguous features create an aura of intrigue and invitation: he's that one college roommate you liked but never partied with, the quiet guy in the office with the cool moped, the funny best friend you'd happily let hang out with your girl. In a word, Bundick is really, really chill.

In fact, the word "chill" has come to define Bundick, referencing far more (and accurately describing far less) than his outward appearance and mannerisms. When the young singer/songwriter/producer started emailing bloggers his homegrown electro experiments in 2008, he was unwittingly claiming real estate in a small renaissance of bedroom producers turning fuzzed-out synths, lush ambience, and

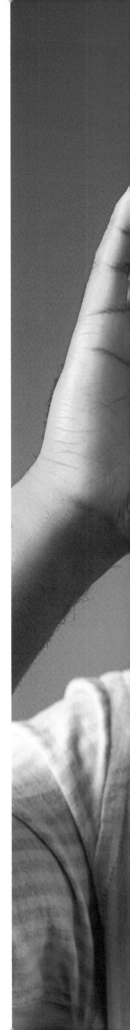

The term "chillwave" has become a four-letter word to some, but when asked about his thoughts on the half- genre, Bundick responds in the only way he knows: "It's all good."

half-sung, reverb-drenched hooks into a palette for nostalgic summers on the beach and blunted nights in Williamsburg, Brooklyn. Rising bands like Neon Indian, Washed Out, and Memory Tapes were being championed by the particularly ruthless indie blogosphere and capturing the imaginations of jaded twenty-somethings across the country. By the time Bundick's "Blessa" hit the web and became his breakout single under the name Toro y Moi, the "chillwave" genre had taken full form and would cause controversy every time it was discussed among listeners and artists alike. Were these indie-everymen true musicians or just hipsters pandering to 1980s retrospective projections? Was there redeemable songwriting hidden beneath the gallons of echoey vocals? Was it all just a big ball of irony mocking the DIY infrastructure that birthed it? And, damn it, how could all these guys be so chill? YouTube commenters debated fiercely, bands were forced to take a side, and the *Wall Street Journal* profiled the key members of the scene—Bundick included—hilariously asking "Is Chillwave the Next Big Music Trend?" The term has become a four-letter word to some, but when asked about his thoughts on the half-genre, Bundick responds in the only way he knows: "It's all good."

It's no surprise that the title doesn't faze him. Toro y Moi escaped from 2010's "Summer of Chillwave" unscathed, and has emerged as one of the most exhilarating artists in the indie music scene. Boasting an intoxicating sound comprised of heavy low-ends, funky rhythms, ambient riffs, and a charming falsetto, his best songs immediately trigger swaying hips and deep grins

from any sound body within earshot. As a songwriter, he is indebted to the sentimentalism of classic R&B and the arcane escapism of alternative rock: deceptively huge hooks burst between verses that tackle broken hearts and bare pockets, landing squarely on the narrow frequency between apathy and insecurity that only his fellow Millennials can hear. "There was a finer life when I was with my friends, and I could always see my family," he sings on 2011's "Still Sound," before finally exhaling, "'Cause I don't want to be alone." His blend of genres might be overwhelming if it weren't for the thread that keeps his sound consistent: an airy, conversational singing voice that floats perfectly through his lush clouds of disco, funk, and psychedelic chords. It's a sound Bundick's been honing in his bedroom for the past decade and that has now swept young music lovers searching for more than commercial pop's four chords—not bad, considering he almost didn't pursue music at all.

Chazwick Bundick was born on November 7, 1986, in Columbia, South Carolina, to an African American father and Filipino mother. He got his first piano lesson at eight years old ("My mom made me play—Asian parents") and was tinkering with the guitar by thirteen. But it wasn't until his sophomore year at Ridgeview High School that music began to shape his daily life and social circle. "My friends and I would play covers," he says of his early days. "We'd cover bands like Weezer and the Pixies, the Ramones, stuff like that. We were just messing around. Sophomore year, we turned into a legitimate band—pop influenced, like if you mixed the Pixies with At the Drive-In." His

As a songwriter, Bundick is indebted to the sentimentalism of classic R&B and the arcane escapism of alternative rock: deceptively huge hooks burst between verses that tackle broken hearts and bare pockets, landing squarely on the narrow frequency between apathy and insecurity that only his fellow Millennials can hear.

crew eventually morphed into the Heist and the Accomplice, a punk band that stirred a local buzz with the 2008 single "More Control." Bundick played front man then, and when the band disintegrated, he kept recording on a four-track his parents bought him. "They're big-time supporters," Bundick says of his parents, former New York City scenesters with an extensive record collection he's recently inherited. "They were always playing music in the house, and I was always listening to what they were playing. My dad likes Joe Jackson and a lot of that English new-wave stuff. Like English Beat and General Public. My mom was more Madonna and Michael Jackson. My dad was a fan of the Specials and stuff. He was more open-minded and open to things that were less popular."

Their eccentric tastes rubbed off on Bundick, who spent his teenage years searching for the obscure music the radio largely ignored. "When I was an angsty teenager all against mainstream music, I'd always be like, 'Oh, everything's the same chords,' so that's really what drew me to find music that sounded a little bit weirder," he explains. "I've always appreciated all kinds of music, but it took me a while to learn about stuff from the past really. I found out older music was influencing bands I was really into. Lounge music influences Broken Social Scene, and then you have bossa nova stuff that influences Yo La Tengo. Once I found out what they were influenced by, I just started getting more into that." The mix of inspirations swirling in Bundick's library eventually grew into the sonic experiments he was honing in his bedroom.

As guitar-driven singer/songwriter tunes gave way to sample-based groove theories, Bundick's interest in record collecting grew stronger. "Whatever genre it is, I'm always looking for chords. That kind of stuff always appealed to me. I liked the obscureness of it. Chord progressions and cool album covers."

With parents funding his college education and not much of a thriving scene in the South, Bundick chose to finish school while tentatively trying out recording as a solo artist. "Wanting to do music was always in the back of my mind. But your parents are always like, 'You've got to be serious about this. Do you really want to do that?' So I had to go to school and get my backup plan situated. Once I started seeing a trend of how bands were getting popular, I started sending my music out over the Internet, and then it started growing."

Blogs began picking up Bundick's loose singles and innovative remixes, and his buzz hit critical mass in June 2009 with "Blessa," a thumping, ambient jam that Ian Cohen of Pitchfork Media describes as "a direct line between the escapism of homemade electro-pop and the lives of the people creating it." The track, which features the prominent chorus "I found a job, I do it fine, do it fine/ Not what I want, but still I try, still I try," resonated strongly with emerging adults living check to check in a dismal economy. He signed with indie label Carpark Records right after graduating college, expecting nothing more than to release some music and hoping that people enjoyed it. "I still try not to expect things," he says. "If something doesn't happen and you expected it, you're

all messed up. We did an album-by-album deal, and I just keep working with them because I like them so much."

Bundick's first release on Carpark, *Causers of This*, was released to critical acclaim in the winter of 2010, with *NME* calling it a "stylishly soporific…blissed-out masterpiece." The project was notably laden with raw emotion—while recording it, Bundick was going through what he calls the most emotionally confused point of his life. "I'd call that my break-up album," he explains. "I had a girlfriend for a really long time, and it just ended. I was in between: 'Am I going to get a design job or do this music thing that could possibly fail?' I was in a zone where I wasn't really hanging out with people or talking to people. I locked myself in my room, just hid away, and worked on stuff." His pain is tangible throughout the album: on "Fax Shadow," the first song he recorded for the project, he sings, "I don't want to know more about him… I'm sorry I couldn't name the color of your eyes." The line was inspired by a real-life exchange with his ex: "We were talking on the phone, and she was like, 'I don't know if I even want to do this anymore… Do you even know what color my eyes are?' And I was like, 'Yeah…'" He pauses, still visibly affected by the relationship. "It was totally embarrassing and made me look like an asshole. But we were both confused. That song is about the time that I went to visit her, and she had already started seeing someone else. It was just a weird time to be making that album."

While emotive songwriting was an obvious strength, it was the production on *Causers* that captivated music lovers across demographics. The album seamlessly blends the ambience of indie rock, the hard grooves of electronic dance music, and the lush samples of classic backpacker hip-hop. Tracks melt into each other through intricate transitions of synth and snare, and pulsing standouts like "Talamak" and "Low Shoulder" lay syrupy textures over fat beats, enrapturing hip-hop heads and punk pundits alike.

"I was listening to a lot of J Dilla and My Bloody Valentine when I made *Causers*," he explains of the album's rare dichotomy. "It's more just little snippets that are peppered throughout. What I wanted to take from Dilla is the atmosphere of it. Listening to his music, you always feel like it swallows you. I wanted to emulate that. And also, I loved the ambience that My Bloody Valentine had. I wanted to make something that was kind of mixed." He began touring the album the summer after graduating and found validation on the road that he couldn't sense on the web—he could actually make a living doing music. "Carpark hooked me up with some merch, and it was selling out. It was enough for me to live on until the next tour. The cost of living is pretty low in the South."

Where *Causers* served as the chillwave landmark, *Underneath the Pine* has quickly become Bundick's defining project. Shedding his Reason sampling software, he recorded his sophomore album entirely live, playing every instrument himself and touring with a live band. The move was received with mixed reactions by those who were expecting more sample-driven electronica from the multifaceted producer, but the album was critically acclaimed and helped raise his profile even further. "I wanted to show people that I wasn't just sampling, and

that I wasn't just some kid with a laptop," he says of the choice to go live. "Whenever I saw [the documentary] *Never Say Never* and Justin Bieber was on drums, I was like, 'Woah.' I can respect that. And performing, when I was doing the laptop stuff onstage, I wasn't feeling it as much as [when] I was performing with the band. It made the live show better to have musicians."

The switch in production also allowed him to experiment with his musical first love: funk. "I'm always going to throw a little bit of funkiness into it," he says. "I can't not do that. The funk and the pop elements are my favorite. From weird, like Lonnie Liston Smith, like astral jazz, to Michael Jackson. I find something really awesome about the chord progressions, and the overall evolution, how it came from jazz. That's crazy. If I could do anything, it would be playing jazz or psychedelic funk forever. That stuff is so good to me."

"New Beat" and his follow-up single "Still Sound" were significantly more accessible than Bundick's work on *Causers*, featuring sugary vocal harmonies, funk backbeats and huge choruses. The singles gained rotation on MTV, played in trendy stores like Urban Outfitters, and began perking the ears of influential music publications and artists. Bundick found scores of new fans and admits that he had larger mainstream aspirations when working on his sophomore LP.

"When I was making *Underneath the Pine*, I wanted to just take my favorite elements of the last album and sort of increase them. I wanted to make some singles that were going to help more R&B/hip-hop listeners transition and become interested in the other side of the spectrum. So it's cool

to see all the sneaker-heads getting into it." One professed fan put many of his sneaker-head admirers on to Toro y Moi: Tyler, the Creator—leader of the rap collective Odd Future—has called Bundick a "fucking genius." "I'd love to work with Tyler. We've already talked about it; we're just both busy," Bundick says. "I wouldn't want to be in a room by myself making a beat and selling it off. If I ever did any collaboration, I would like them to be in the studio, artist with another artist."

Coming up in the indie world has its own hardships, particularly with bands being pigeonholed to certain sounds, and accusations of "selling out" flying rampantly from critics and bloggers. Having found a decent amount of success, Bundick still places the music before all politics. "As an artist, if you're as far as I've come, you want to be commercially successful and respected by all. If you look at artists like Arcade Fire, they won a Grammy for Album of the Year and did a great job of breaking that whole realm of Pitchfork artists. It just shows you've just got to do what you've got to do if you still want to make good music and prove people wrong sometimes. But I'm still not trying to be a super famous pop star. If it happens, it happens."

With a new dance EP just hitting the web, a nationwide tour, and plans for a new album, Chaz Bundick is hoping to finally take a bit of a break. "It's always hectic," he vents before hopping onstage. "When the tour ends, I think I'm planning on taking a good amount of time just to write songs at a normal pace and have my life back for a second." And who can blame him? After all, everybody needs a moment to chill. ●

Photo by Jorge Peniche.

RECORD RUNDOWN
DJ Quik

by **Tony Best**

MC and producer DJ Quik emerged in the late-1980s as a versatile and prolifc hip-hop force from Compton, California. Having shaped the sound of West Coast rap with his rubber-band-funk-laced beats, Quik picks from a broad spectrum of music that has informed his scientific approach to music.

"When you sample," says Compton, California, legend DJ Quik, "it's more than just about the musical piece. It's the *wow* and *flutter* from the turntable. There's something about the electrified diamond touching the carbon-based vinyl that makes the sound so robust. The concept shouldn't even work. It's a miracle of physics, if you ask me."

DJ Quik (né David Blake) tends to pepper his musical discussions with scientific and mathematical terminologies. And that's not much of a stretch. With a lauded twenty-plus-year discography, the self-styled mad scientist not only sonically alchemizes disparate genres—from '80s synth-boogie to Bollywood melodies—but also surreptitiously infuses his beats with concepts of synesthesia ("you can hear colors in my music") and audio field equation theory. Pretty heady stuff for G-funk, but think Carl Sagan rocking two Technics and an MPC60.

Wax Poetics caught up with Quik at L.A.'s Amoeba Music on June 7, 2011 (Prince's fifty-third birthday), where the West Coast auteur methodically dug through vinyl bins in search of both obscure and nostalgic records recalled from his Compton childhood. Quik was also conducting aural research for three upcoming projects: the debut LP from protégé Gift Reynolds, a reunion with Richard Pryor–incarnate Suga Free, and his ninth solo album, which according to Quik, will likely be his final hip-hop offering.

◐1

Prince
The Hits/The B-Sides
(Paisley Park/Warner Bros.)
1993

Love this man and his music. I bought every Prince album. But the first two [*For You* and *Prince*] are essential must-haves. And the records he produced as Jamie Starr and the Starr Company. My favorite slow song is "Adore," but every ballad he had on his albums was smokin'. That's when motherfuckers was into ballads. "Do Me, Baby" was before I hit puberty, so I didn't get it. But when I got pubertal, I got it then. [*laughs*] My favorite up-tempo record is "Erotic City"—a slick-ass record, jack. "Head," "Housequake"…two other funky, fast Prince records. I even tried to sample "Let's Work" [from *Controversy*], but it was too hyper; I couldn't make it funky.

◐2

The Beatles
Sgt. Pepper's Lonely Hearts Club Band
(Parlophone) 1967

I bought this record numerous times. I like it for what it was—a fucking crazy piece of art. The way they put it together was uncanny. Crazy editing, crazy tape effects. Cutting pieces together to make sense. Some highly creative, brilliant shit. It's like the *Willy Wonka* record of their catalog. They were in their trippy zone, either shrooming or on LSD. You can hear it in the music, and it's a wonderful thing to listen to sober. It's up there with *Thriller* to me. One of the greatest records of all time.

◐3

Minnie Riperton
Love Lives Forever
(Capitol) 1980

Minnie Riperton can sing *anyone* under the table. But I also had this record because I liked to look at her big, pretty face on the cover. This right here, "Here We Go"—one of the greatest records ever. Vocals done with Roberta Flack and Peabo Bryson. I sampled this song for a radio station drop way back when. And I heard that Patrice Rushen came in and sang some of "The Song of Life" with her because she was sick. Minnie didn't have the chance to finish this album on her own. Check out Michael Jackson on "I'm in Love Again" with Hubert Laws. The Waters Sisters sang some background stuff. A brilliant fucking record. I got this CD in the car. I never stay far away from this album. Minnie *was* music…but she burned too fast.

◐4

Smokey Robinson
A Quiet Storm
(Tamla) 1975

"Baby That's Backatcha" is hot. "The Agony and the Ecstasy," "Quiet Storm," these records are…pure soul. Soul was indefinable back then; the masses didn't really know what it was. You either had it or you didn't. It was esoteric, like a secret handshake. It was more of a Black movement. It was Black people, moving in time, doing exactly what other Black people all across America were doing. And we were all synced up by that great clock, *Soul Train*. Now, everybody's just scatterbrain—no more unity or cohesiveness.

○5

The Doors
L.A. Woman
(Elektra) 1971

Hot record. I like "Crawling King Snake." I sampled "Riders on the Storm" a few times on some shit. And "L.A. Woman" is just the epitome of fucking roadhouse blues. [*sings chorus*] Jim Morrison had a thing, man. Transfixing—he was a fucking superstar. Dude was a shaman, a witch doctor with the music.

○6

Al Green
Let's Stay Together
(Hi) 1972

My mother and this record… she played "I've Never Found a Girl (Who Loves Me Like You Do)" so much that the grooves got burned off. It literally didn't play anymore. She went to put it on one time and the needle just went [*scratch*] right into the next song. She used to put that record on and dance *hard*. It was one of those '70s-soul Black-women things. But Al went platinum every time back then, singing his ass off.

○7

Hiroshima
Hiroshima
(Arista) 1979

One of my favorite groups ever. This song "Lion Dance" was dope. "Never, Ever" was dope and "Roomful of Mirrors" is one of the most beautiful ballads ever written. My sisters turned me on to this record back in '79. I loved it the first time I heard it. That koto sound was so new and distinctive. I never heard that instrument on a record back then. And they didn't sound Japanese when you listened to them. They sounded like a dope jazz band from the States.

○8

Leroy Hutson
Hutson II
(Curtom) 1976

Hard record to find on vinyl. This inspired my musical virtuosity, if you will. He's so experimental on this album. This record is really fucking bad. Curtis Mayfield handpicked him as his replacement in the Impressions. Did you know that this album cover was advertised in the movie *Superman II*? It was when they threw Superman into the bus and the crowd said, "Oh my God, they killed Superman. Let's get 'em!" The record was right there in the window, big as shit. I don't know how Leroy Hutson worked that, but he got his money's worth for that advertising!

○9

Millie Jackson
I Had to Say It
(Spring) 1980

My mama used to love this record. Side two: "Gather round, everybody…" Millie was seriously rapping on this, and the shit was fonky. It was hot, like some pre-funk. That bass line—them dudes was cookin'. The session band was some down-South cats from Atlanta. No wonder they was funkin'.

○10

Kraftwerk
Computer World
(Warner Bros.) 1981

This is another record I gotta buy right now. This took hip-hop to a whole other level. But besides "Numbers," this is a difficult album to lift breaks from—I tried so many times. I might be able to get away with it now—meaning, make it make sense. This album is techno-pop, but the tempo made it hot. To me this is pre–Teddy Riley. It's like new jack swing came from this record with those big snares.

KRAFTWERK · COMPUTER WORLD

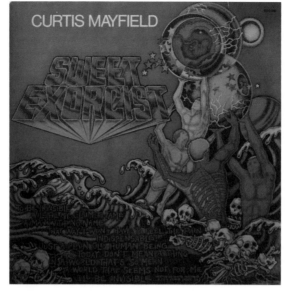

○11

Curtis Mayfield
Sweet Exorcist
(Curtom) 1974

Obviously, this is my favorite musician of all time. Hands down, bar none. This record right here, "Ain't Got Time"— still one of the most incredible records ever. I sampled that for Chingy's "Bagg Up." Dude's album sold three million copies. To me, when Curtis went from just being an artist and became a producer, he went bigger. Then he started scoring movies and became a composer…dope. And check out this artwork. Back then, when it was all about vinyl, you could relate to your favorite artist because of how *big* the pictures were. This shit is life-size.

○12

Malcolm McLaren
"Hobo Scratch (She's Looking Like a Hobo)"
(Island) 1983

This is an incredible 12-inch. I bought this when I was a little kid. The break was incredible. Island Records just had this big sound about them. Huge. Obviously, a lot of people sampled from this, because it's one of a kind. I used a similar clap from this record for "Luv of My Life" [from *The Book of David*]. The clap is kind of special and even proprietary to this particular era. That '80s, New York, cocaine-driven production. But them motherfuckers was funky though.

○13

NWA
"Something 2 Dance 2"
(Ruthless) 1988

Yeah, I had this, but another DJ lifted it from my crates at a party. The song was kind of out of place on the album [*Straight Outta Compton*], like they just threw it out there. But I still like it though. Back then, NWA could do no wrong. But to be honest, some of their later stuff like *Efil4zaggin* was too frenetic for me. It's kind of hard to listen to that particular album. But *Straight Outta Compton* definitely inspired me. I even sampled some of it for my first album [*Quik Is the Name*]. Love them niggas, man.

○14

One Way
"Don't Fight the Feeling"
[white-label promo] (MCA)
1982

I stole this beat for a few of my records. The syncopation of that simple-ass drum break and the way they played that bass line is phenomenal. When you look into it, it's not a simple funk bass line. When you play that scale out, that's some classical shit. [*hums*] It's an incredible song. And for them to cap it with that little triad chord…oh my God! They put that on the *one*! It just makes you geek every time you hear it. Gets into your body, you know? Automatically makes you dance. It tickles your funky bone.

○15

Noel Pointer
Phantazia
(Blue Note) 1977

Believe it or not, the jazz I appreciated was the kind from this dude. He was a Black violinist. I liked this album not just for the breakbeats and loops, even though I did sample some of this for 2nd II None. *Phantazia* is *bam!*—outta here, man. The cut "Night Song" will change your life. Earl Klugh wrote it. Some of the most beautiful music you'll ever hear. My sisters turned me on to this album. Produced by the great Dave Grusin.

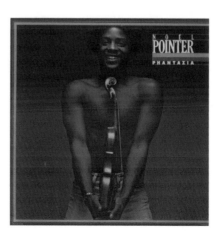

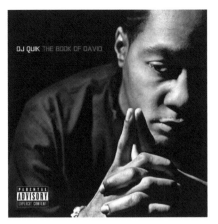

○ 16

Ludwig van Beethoven
Complete Works
(Amado) 2007

I always look for new music so I don't hit a creative brick wall. Because how much more funk and R&B can you sample? It's time hip-hop producers stretch out, go for something bigger. So classical fueled my taste for music, specifically scoring. Who doesn't want to be a dope-ass film scorer and be remembered forever? Dr. Dre is deep into classical now, so we're on the same page. He's trying to broaden his horizons. That's another reason I started researching Beethoven. And it made me realize why a lot of these composers lived short lives. It's got to be hard to maintain stability when you write heavy music that makes people feel like that. And look how much music this mother-fucker wrote. [*lifts the eighty-seven-disc box set*] But even Beethoven was starting to repeat [himself], because there's only twelve notes on the scale.

○ 17

Lee Ritenour
Rit
(Elektra) 1981

This album is my shit right here. A must for anybody trying to become a musician. "Mr. Briefcase," I can play that on the piano. "Is It You?" can be sampled right now and be a hot record. He remade Sly Stone's record, "(You Caught Me) Smilin'." "No Sympathy" is one of the most beautiful ballads ever… It's sad as shit though. If you ever get your heart broken put that mother-fucker on. I guarantee you'll feel better. [*laughs*]

○ 18

DJ Quik
The Book of David
(Mad Science) 2011

I based the sound of this album on classic, seminal '80s records. I used the same vintage equipment and got the same kind of emotive sound. Like if it was recorded at Westlake Audio. I was going for that Bruce Swedien three-dimensional depth when I was mixing this. You have to listen to *The Book of David* a few times to hear everything that's going on. There's a lot of nuances in this album. Check it out on vinyl. There's a lot of movement with the wow and flutter. But I don't know if people are really into that anymore, you know, like art for art's sake? They don't get it. Like I say, my talents are being wasted on hip-hop right now. There are other places where I can be more prominent.

○ 19

Switch
Switch
(Gordy) 1978

One of my favorite R&B records of all time. This record, "I Wanna Be Closer," the one Jermaine Jackson wrote, is the best ballad ever. I'll tell you why. It was Bobby and Tommy DeBarge's voices. Incredible. Bobby had the best falsetto in the business. Period, hands down. Nobody sings that good. The closest is Johnnie Wilder from Heatwave. Both of these dudes took falsetto to another level. It was so pure and had so much range. I'm sure these motherfuckers got the pick of any woman they wanted—damn! They had that look with the permed hair, the press and curl. Where do you think I got it from? I wanted to look like them! **○**

94 East
Minneapolis Genius
(Hot Pink) 1985

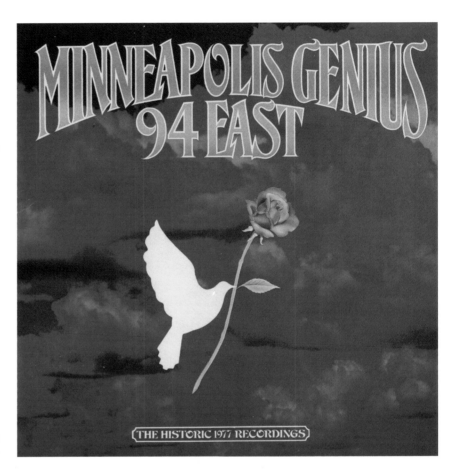

One of the earliest recorded examples of Prince's musicianship is the *Minneapolis Genius* record, credited to 94 East. The album, a paragon of Prince-sploitation, was released in 1985, when *Purple Rain* was in the midst of a twenty-four-week run at the top of the *Billboard* album charts and the eponymous tour was presenting "the pinnacle of the Prince and the Revolution experience," as keyboardist Lisa Coleman put it. The cover bludgeons the viewer with as many oblique Prince references as the art director could get away with, from the *Minneapolis Genius* title (hint: they weren't talking about Bob Dylan) and dove holding a single rose to a background that's a primer on various shades of purple.

With one exception, the LP's songs were cobbled together from two recording sessions, one in 1978 in Minneapolis at the Sound 80 studio and another in early 1979 at New York's Music Farm. Both occasions were under the aegis of Linster "Pepé" Willie, a New Yorker who was Prince's cousin by marriage and for this short window of time the most musically connected member of the family. Pepé Willie's uncle was Clarence Collins, one of the founding members of Little Anthony and the Imperials. The New York session was intended to serve as a demo for Tony Silvester, lead singer of the Main Ingredient, who was slated to produce an LP for the Imperials. Silvester did not find the songs a good fit, and the group returned to Minneapolis empty-handed (the Imperials gig went to Leroy Burgess collaborator Stan Lucas).

Willie himself was a keyboard player, but what he actually contributed to these songs is a matter of conjecture, since Prince is credited with both guitar and synthesizers. The other individual who features heavily here is André Anderson, later to rename himself André Cymone, who played most of the bass parts. The teen Prince Rogers Nelson ("Skippy" to his school friends) had moved in with neighbor André and his mother after leaving his parents' house sometime around 1973. It was shortly after this that he met Willie, who took the boys jam band under his wing. In 1975, he began using them on sessions for his nascent 94 East project, a group he hoped to get signed to Polydor (the LP's earliest cut, "Games," dates from this period).

The 1979 session gave birth to the album's most popular cut, "If You Feel Like Dancing," a favorite of Larry Levan and the Paradise Garage crowd. It was later remixed by house DJ Tony Humphries and issued as a 12-inch single, but the more organic LP version is the preferred take (as evidenced by its inclusion on the notorious *Paradise Garage Classics* bootleg series). The blistering ribbon of lead guitar that unwinds over the course of its seven minutes is testament to the possessed musical imagination belonging to the twenty-one-year-old guitarist.

The tracks were never used for the Imperials, and Willie's wooing of Polydor fell flat. But in 1985, Prince blew up. The odds and ends that had been gathering dust gained new life as the debut of the Minneapolis Genius. ● **Andrew Mason**